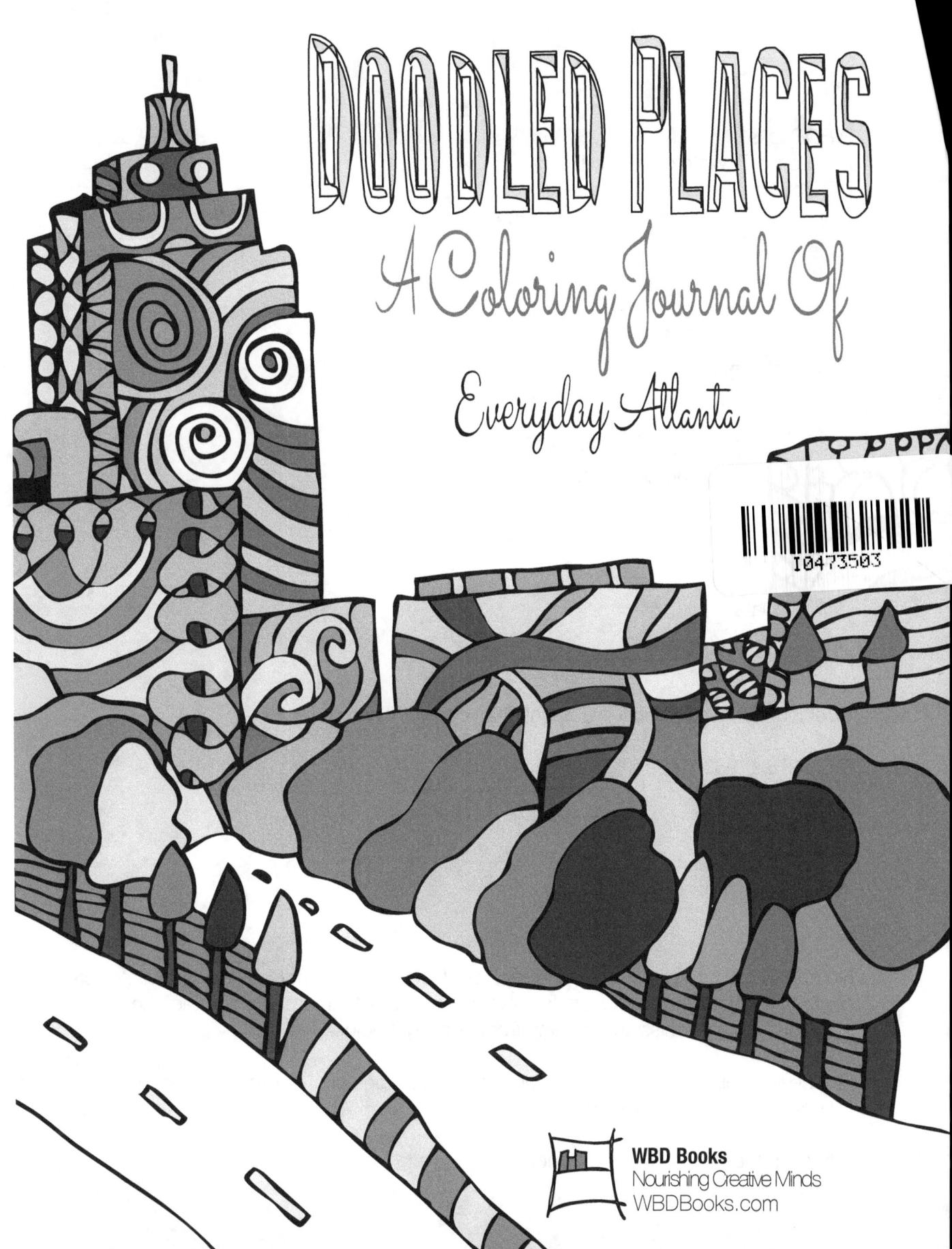

DOODLED PLACES

A Coloring Journal Of

Everyday Atlanta

WBD Books
Nourishing Creative Minds
WBDBooks.com

WBDBooks
An Imprint Of Watercolors By Design
PO Box 51
Duluth, GA 30096 USA
www.wbdbooks.com

FIRST EDITION

First Printing (September 2015)

Catalog Data

Peterson, M

Doodled Places : A Coloring Journal Of Everyday Atlanta

ISBN 978-0-9830451-5-1 Paperback

Printed in the United States of America

DOODLED PLACES

A Coloring Journal Of

Everyday Atlanta

M. PETERSON

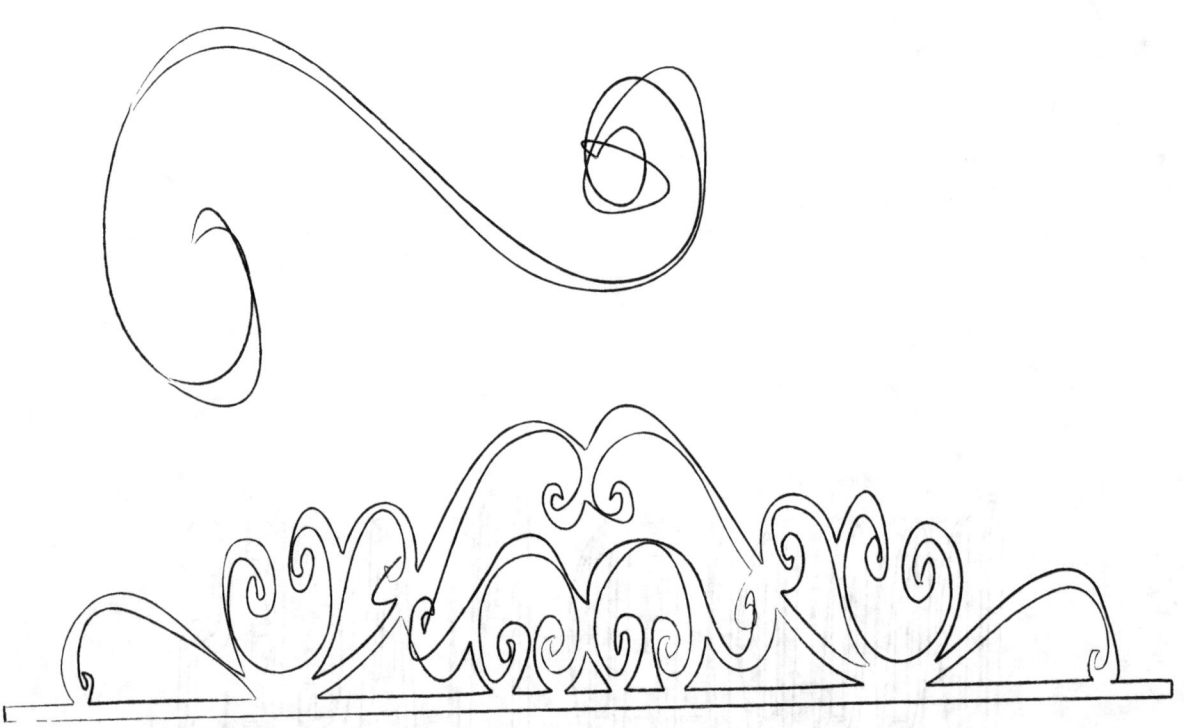

Landscapes with buildings reaching the sky

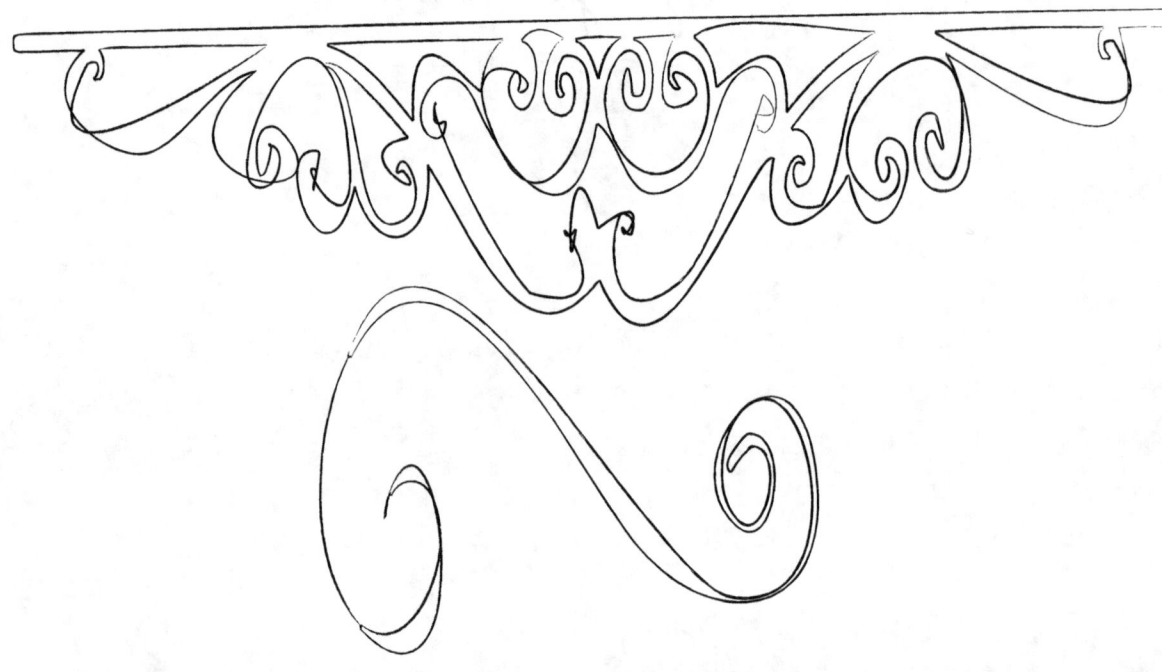

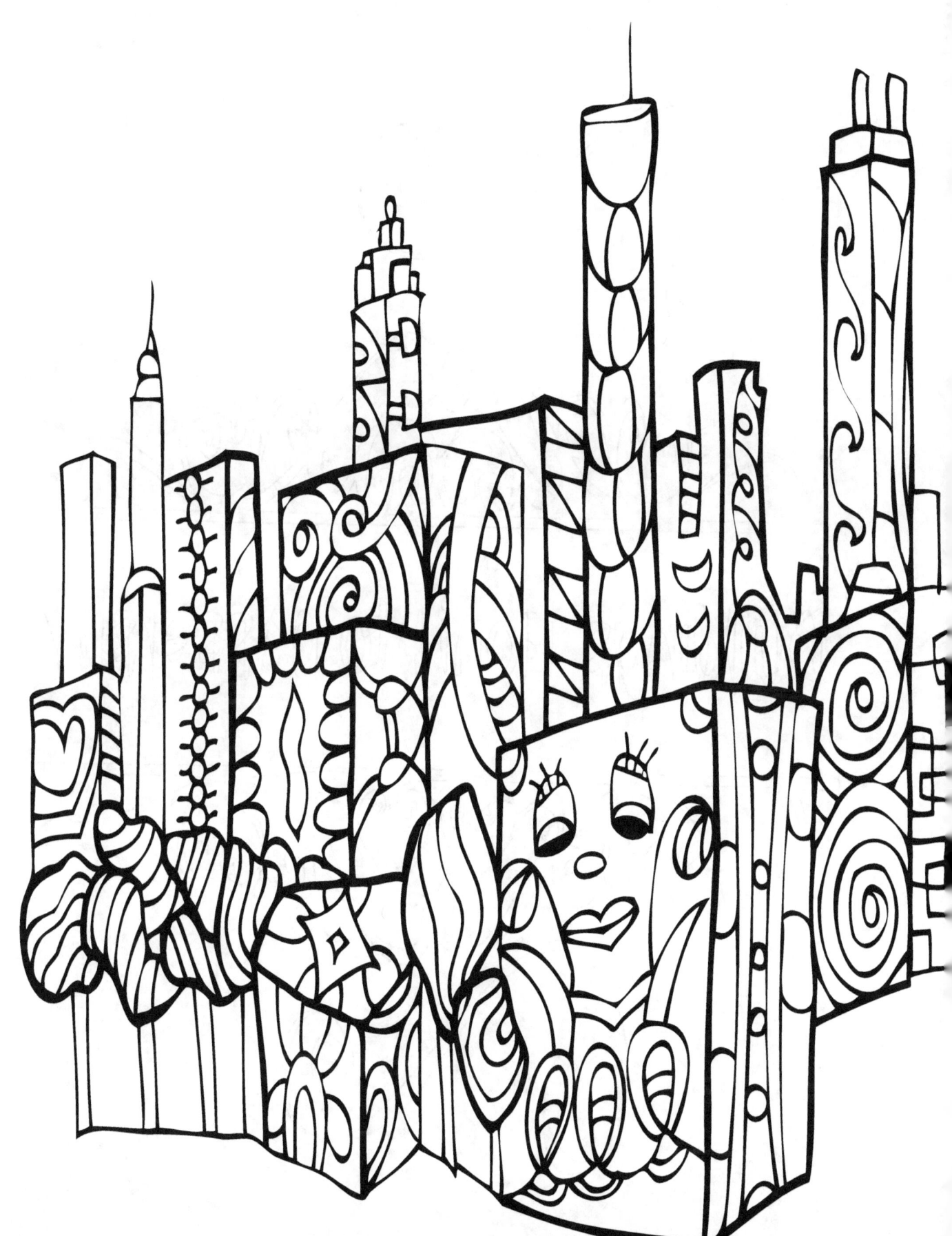

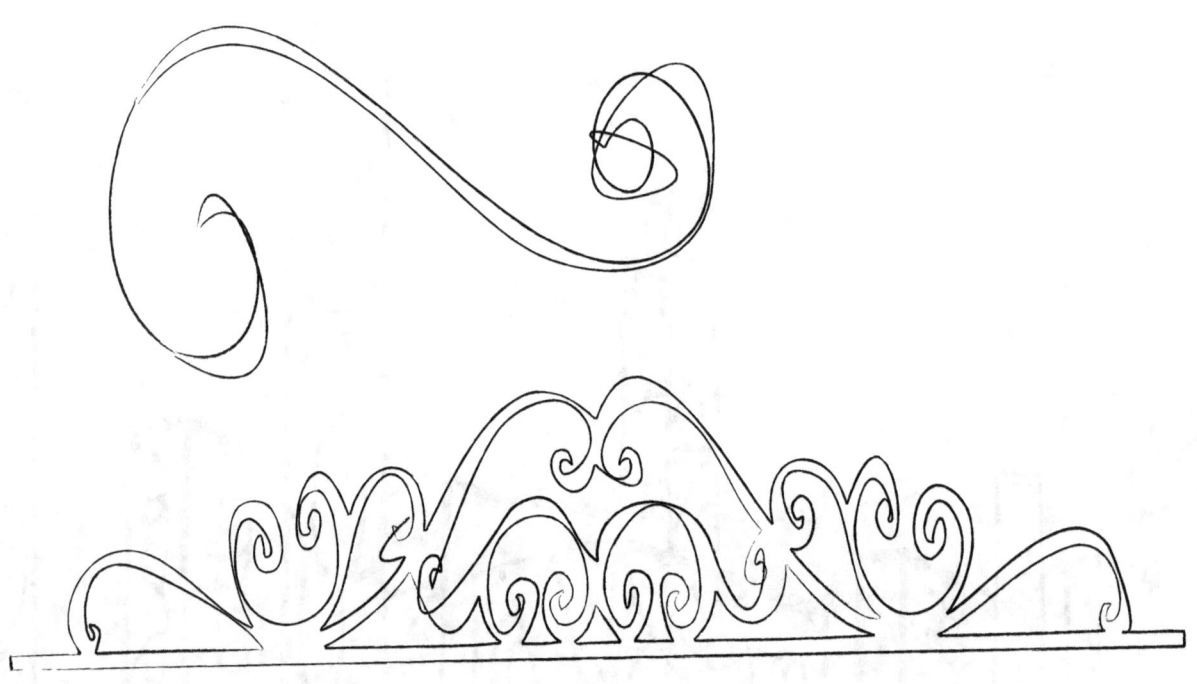

Buildings itonit to passersby

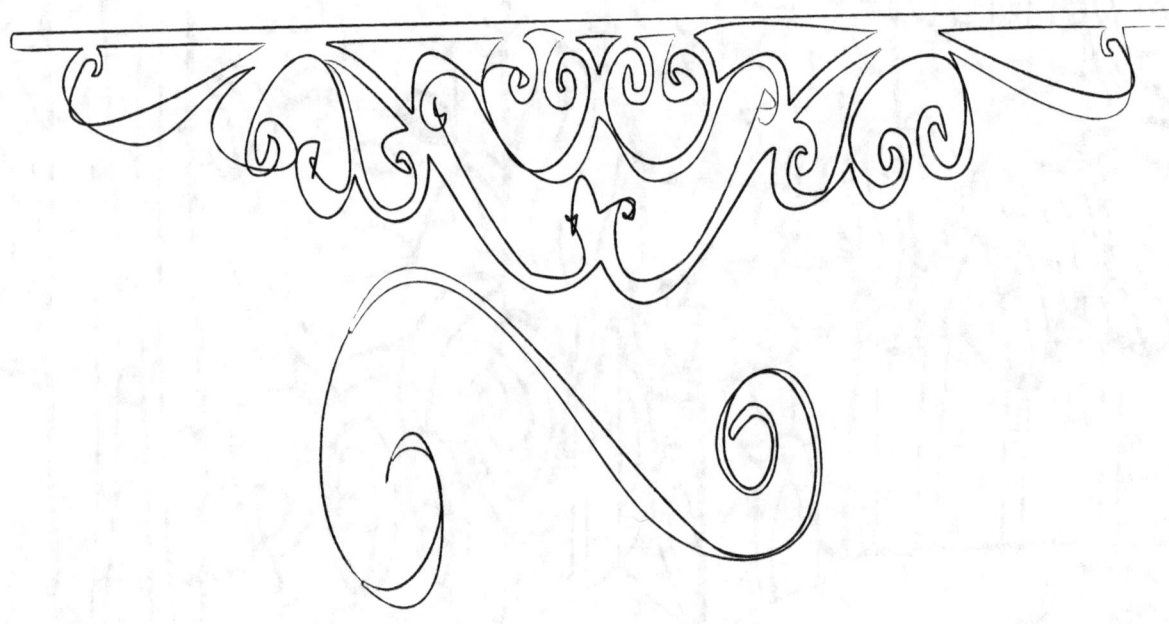

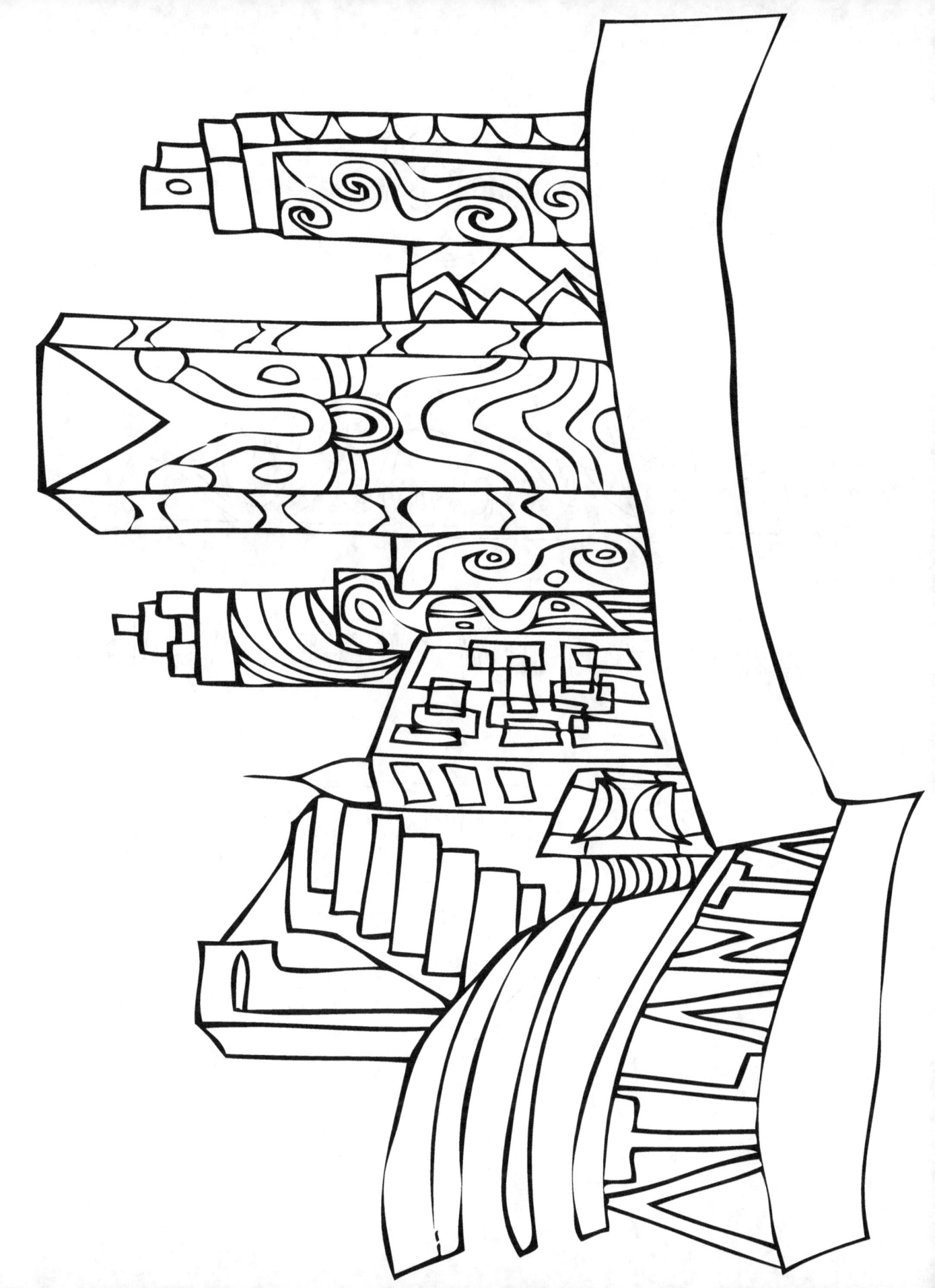

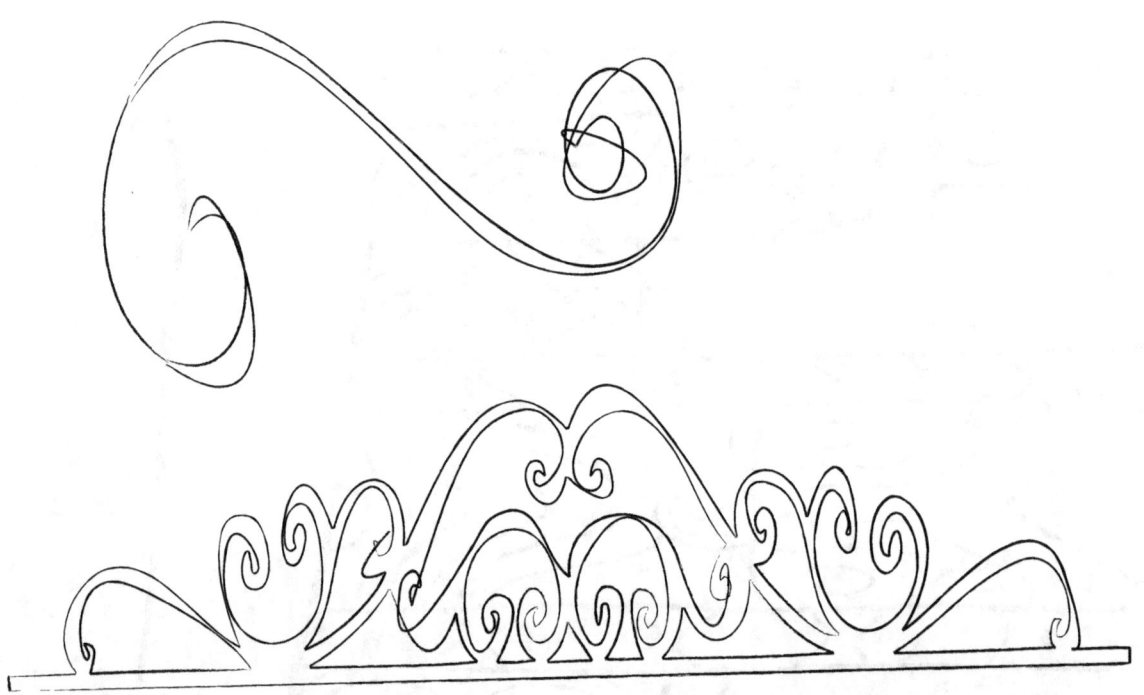

Wild bamboo grows on North Avenue

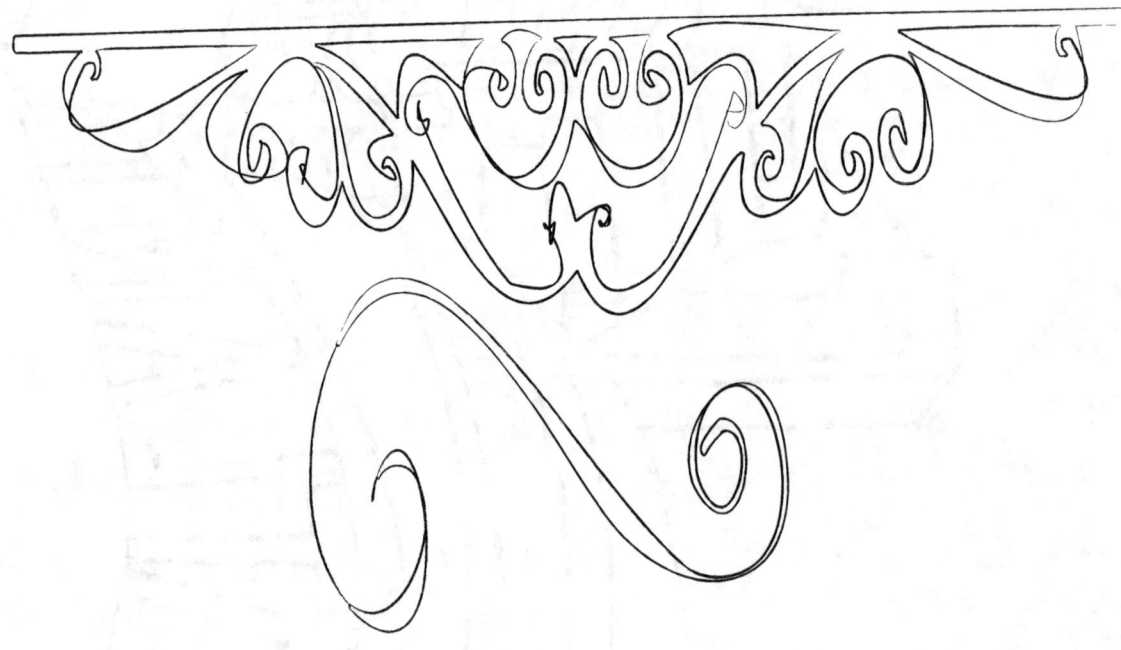

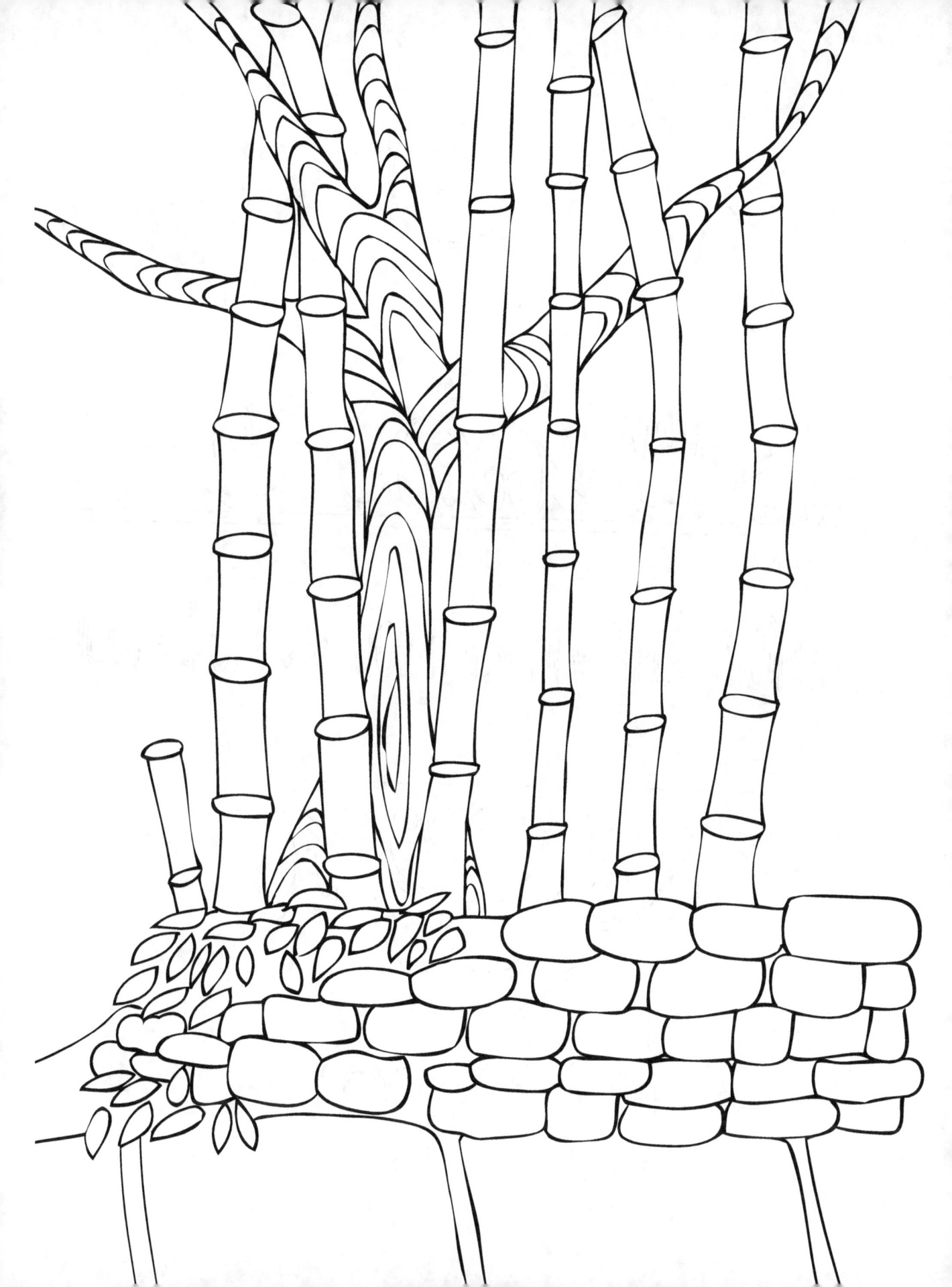

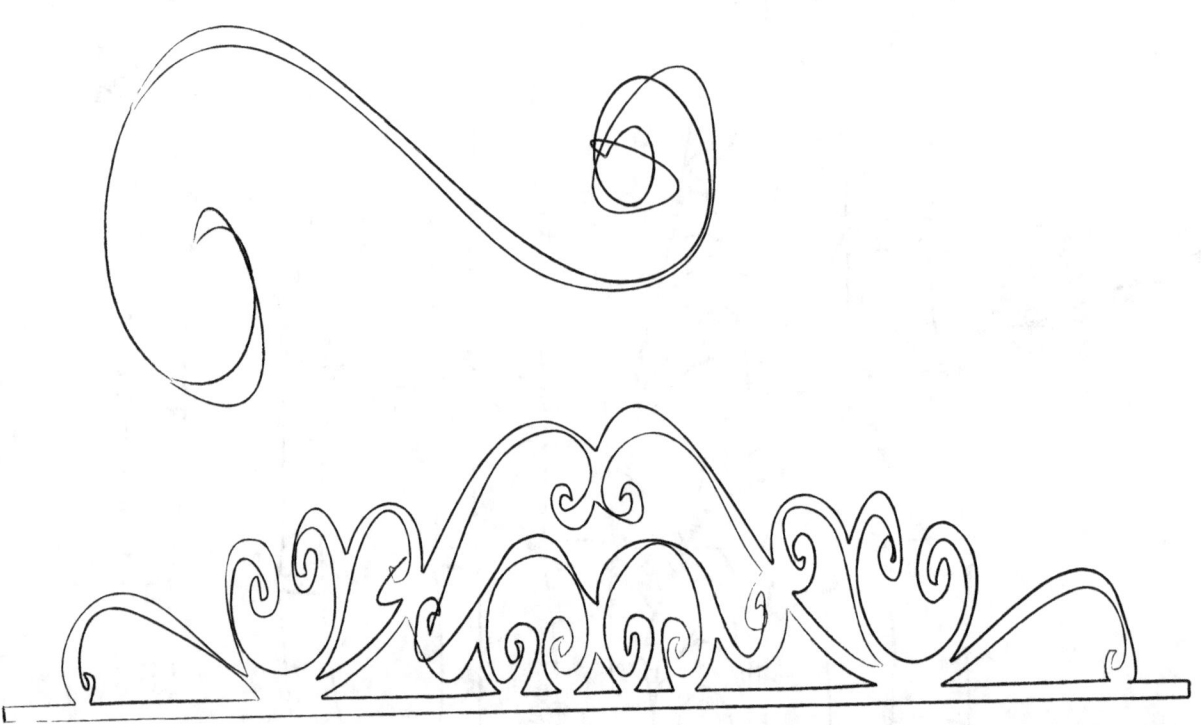

Fountains to play in when you need to be cool

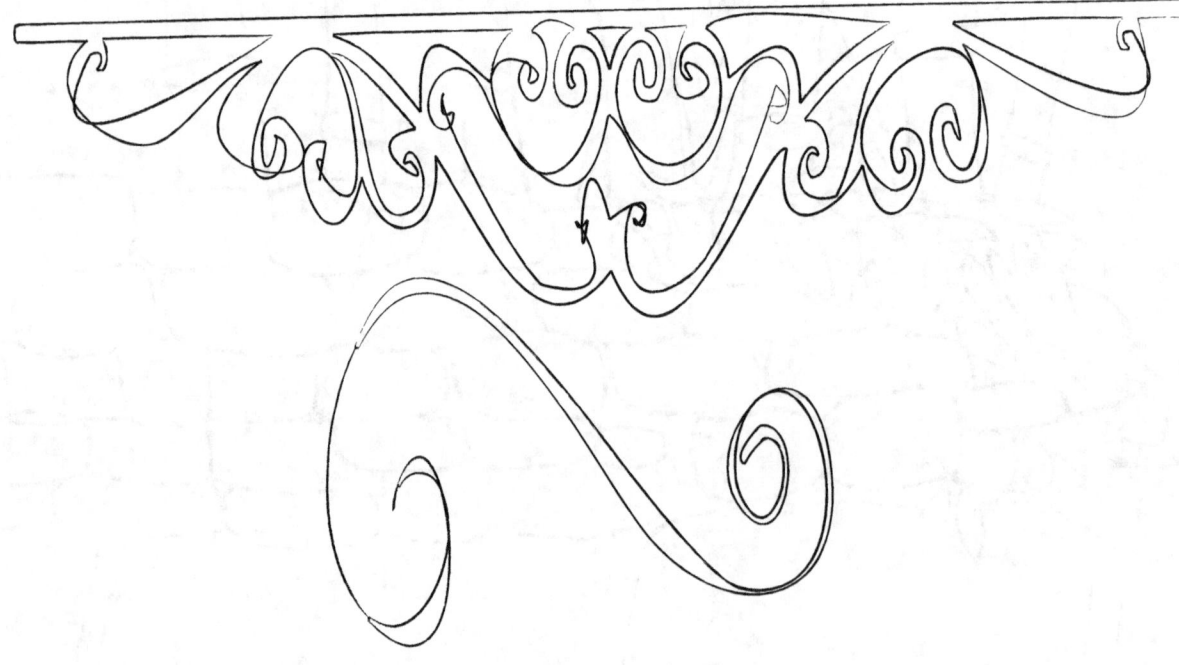

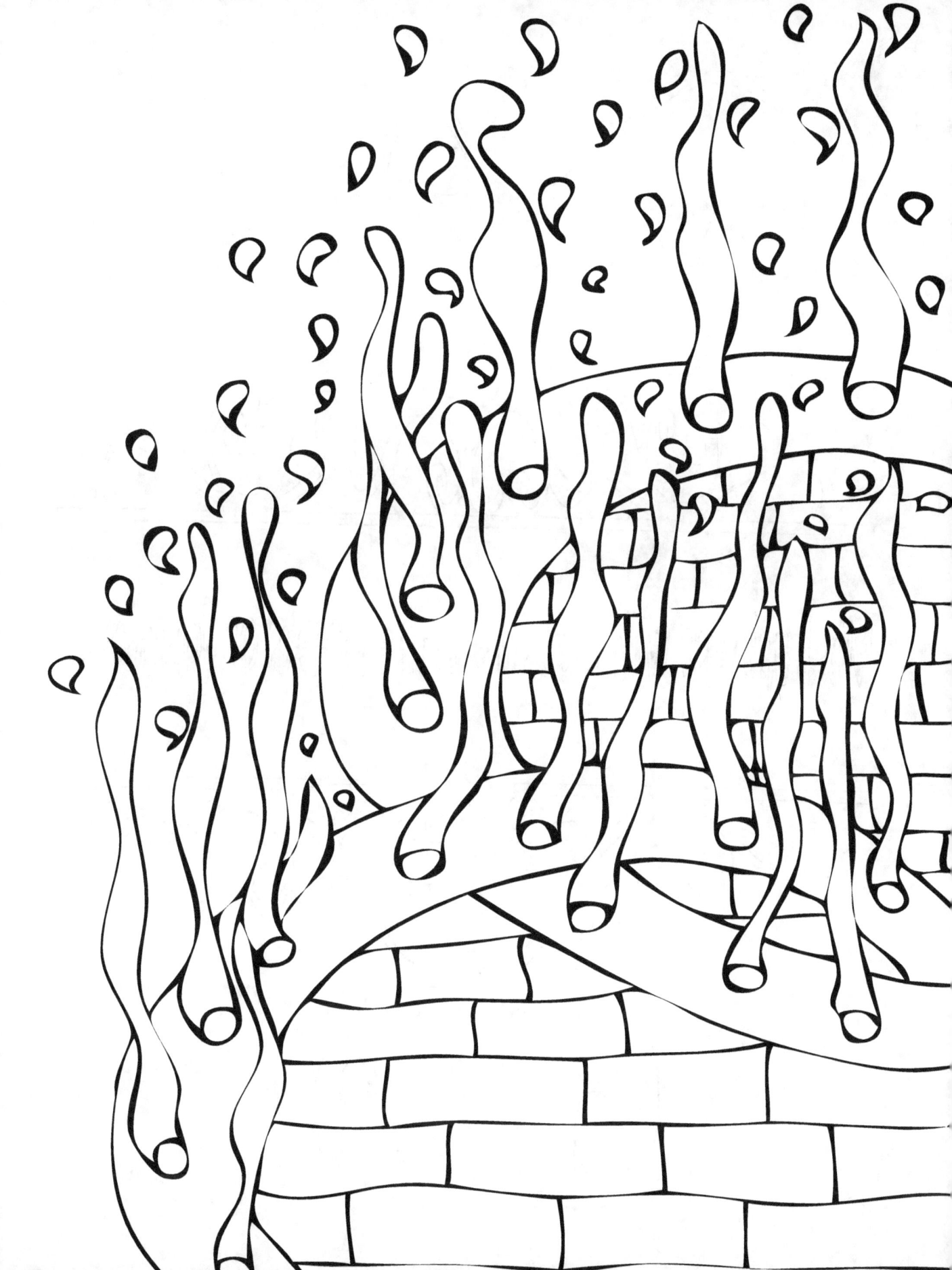

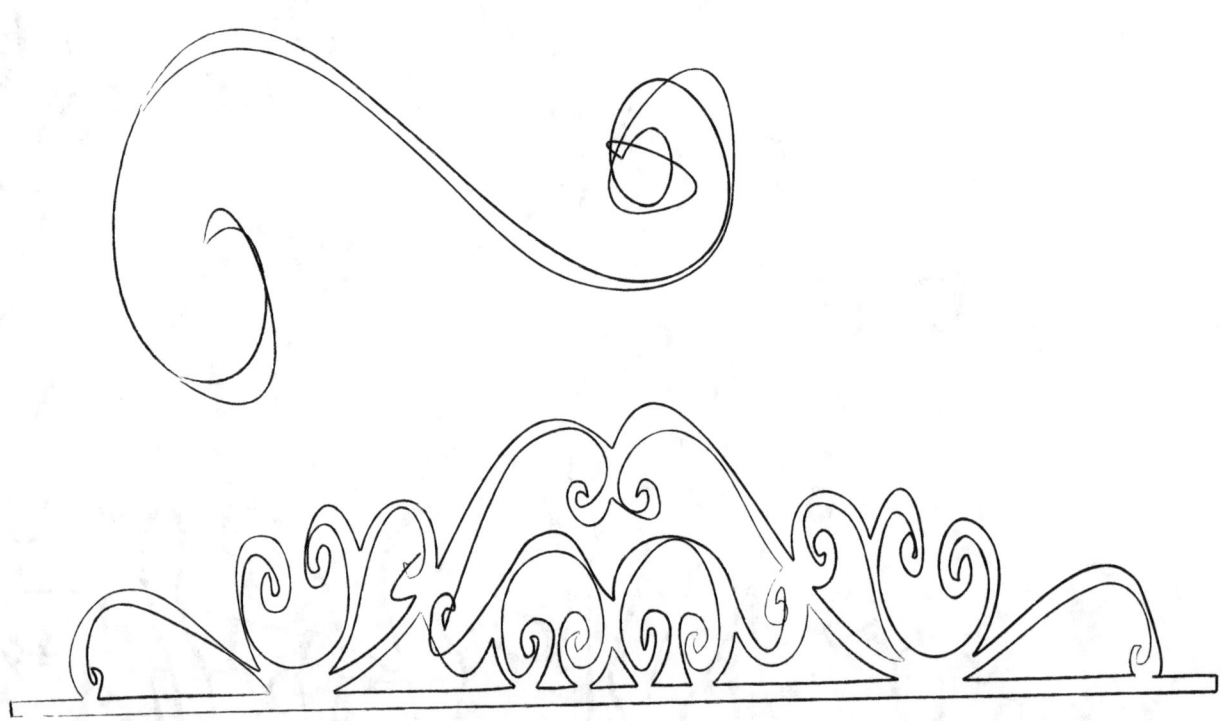

Mix business with pleasure in the streets of downtown

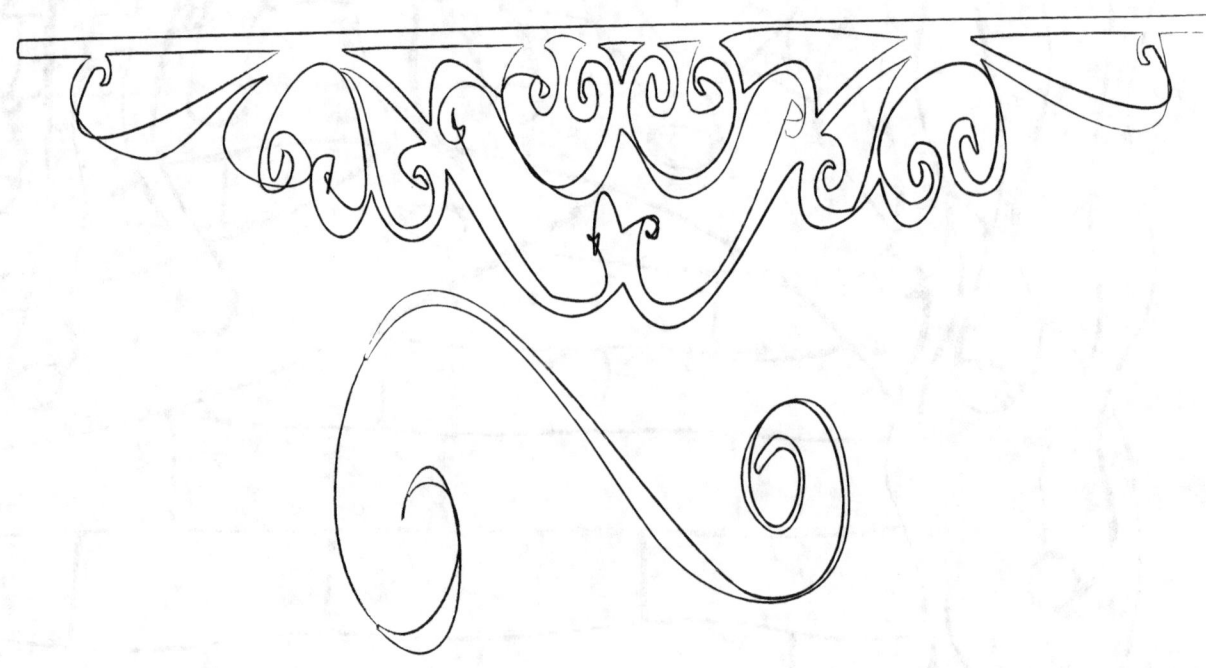

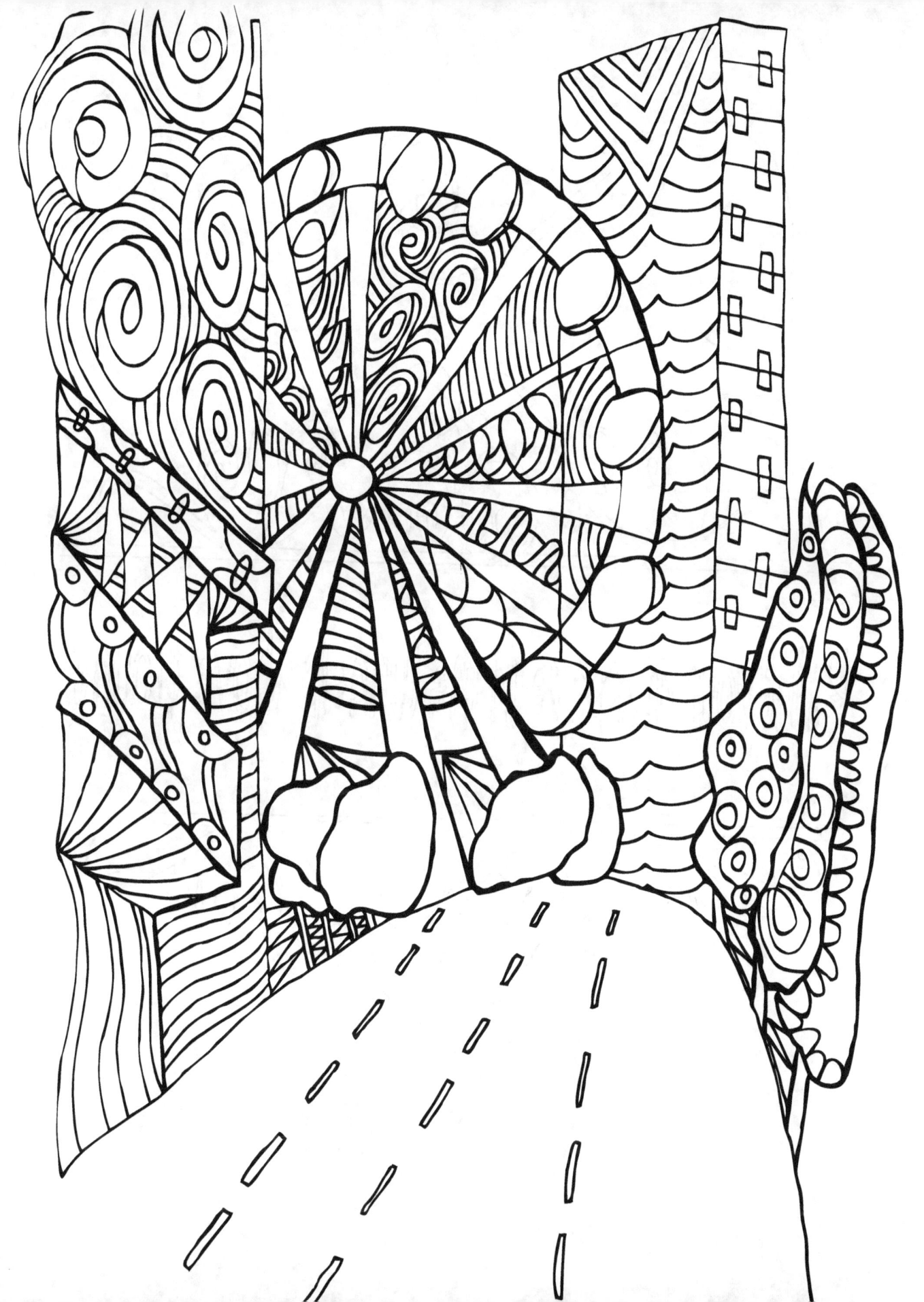

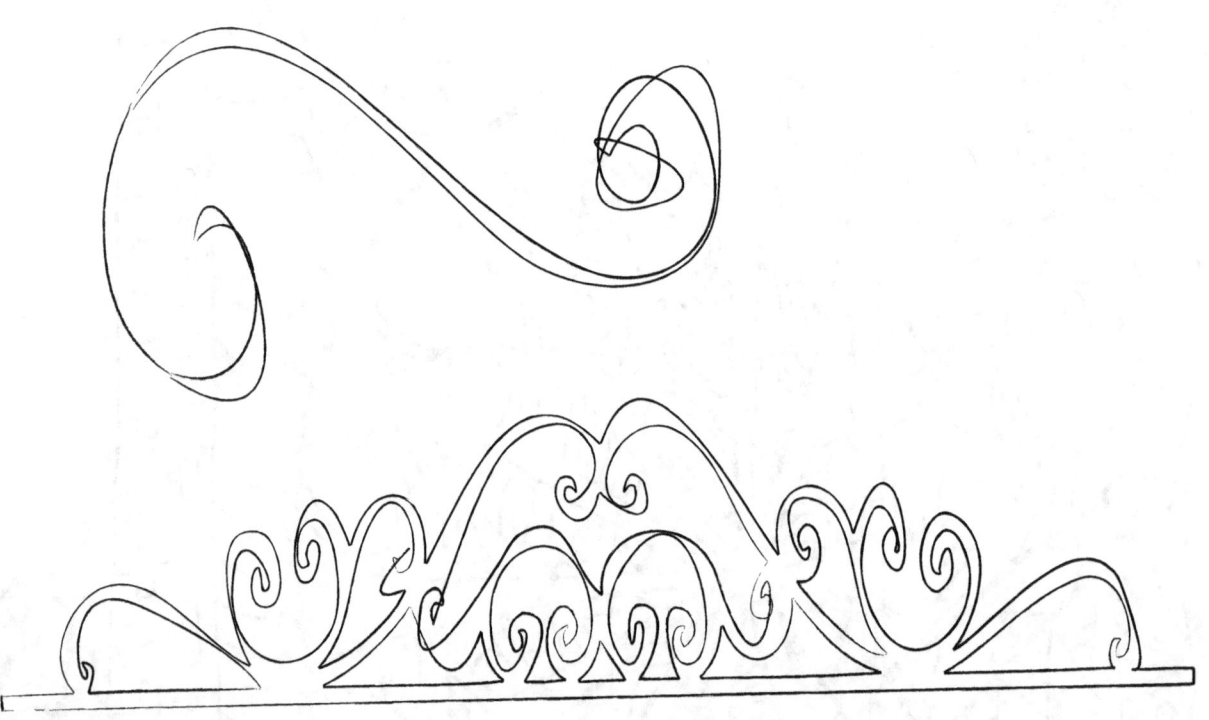

Paint your message in the tunnels above ground

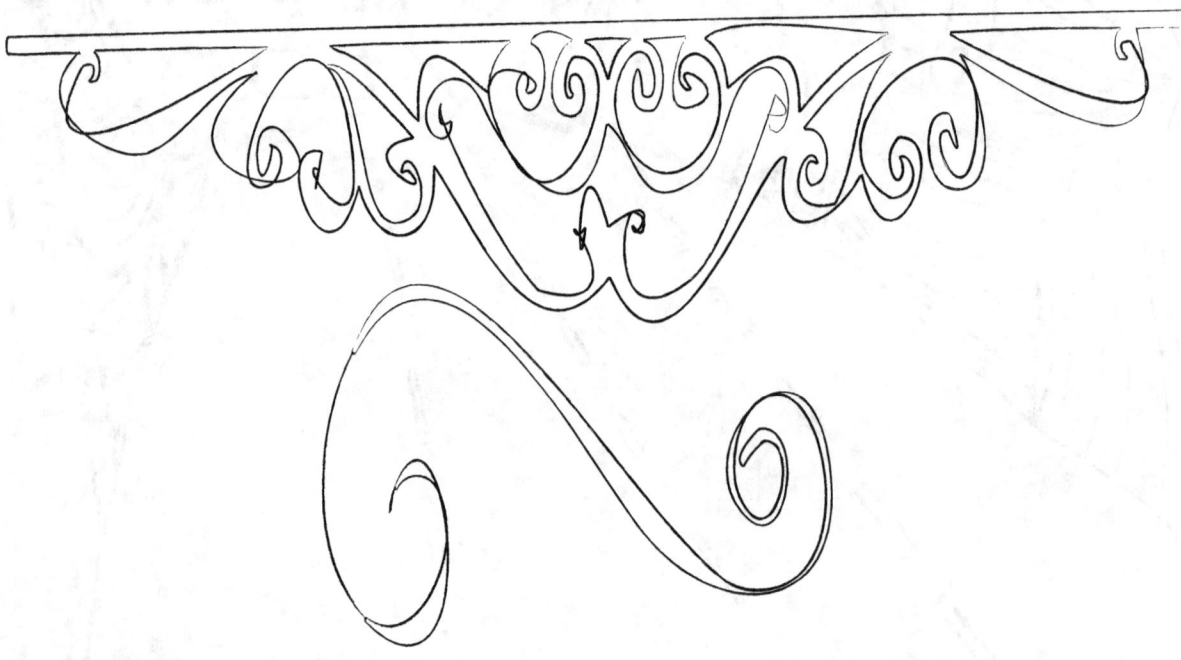

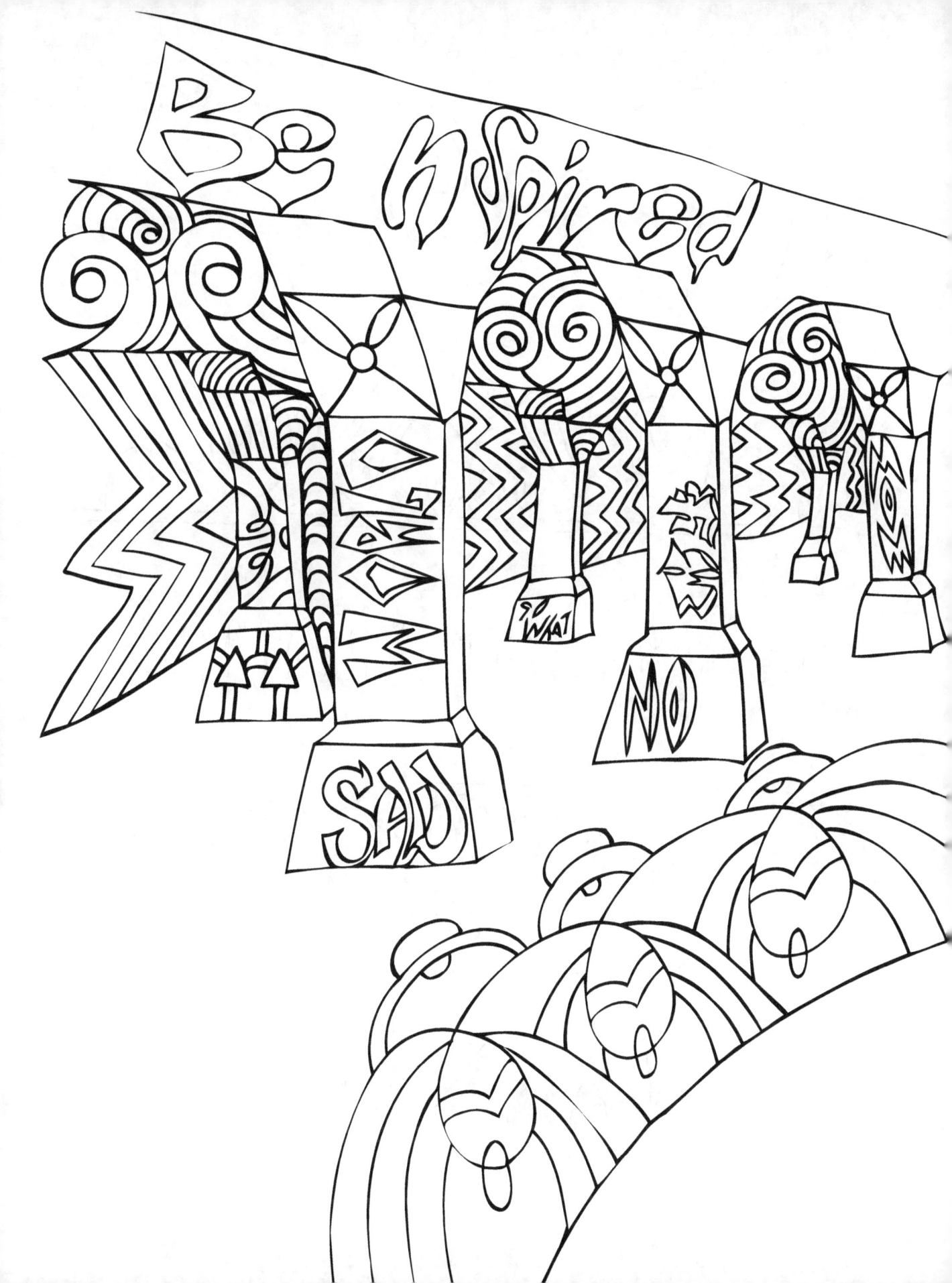

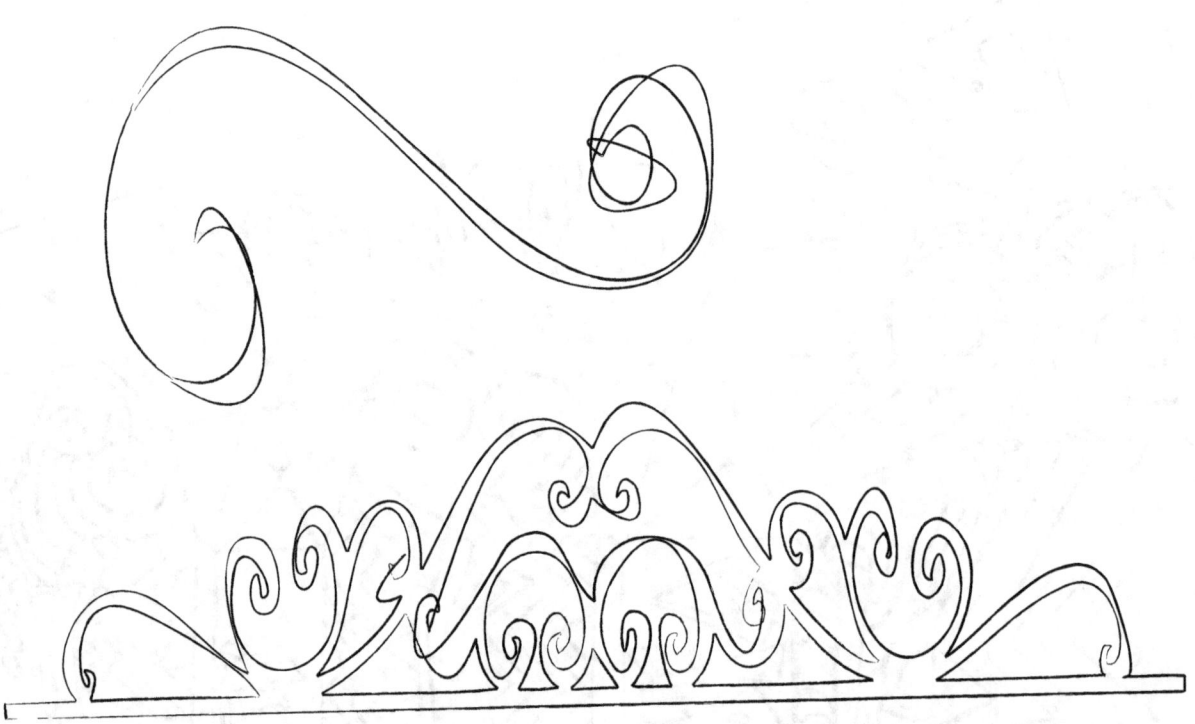

Live like a hipster in Bohemian style

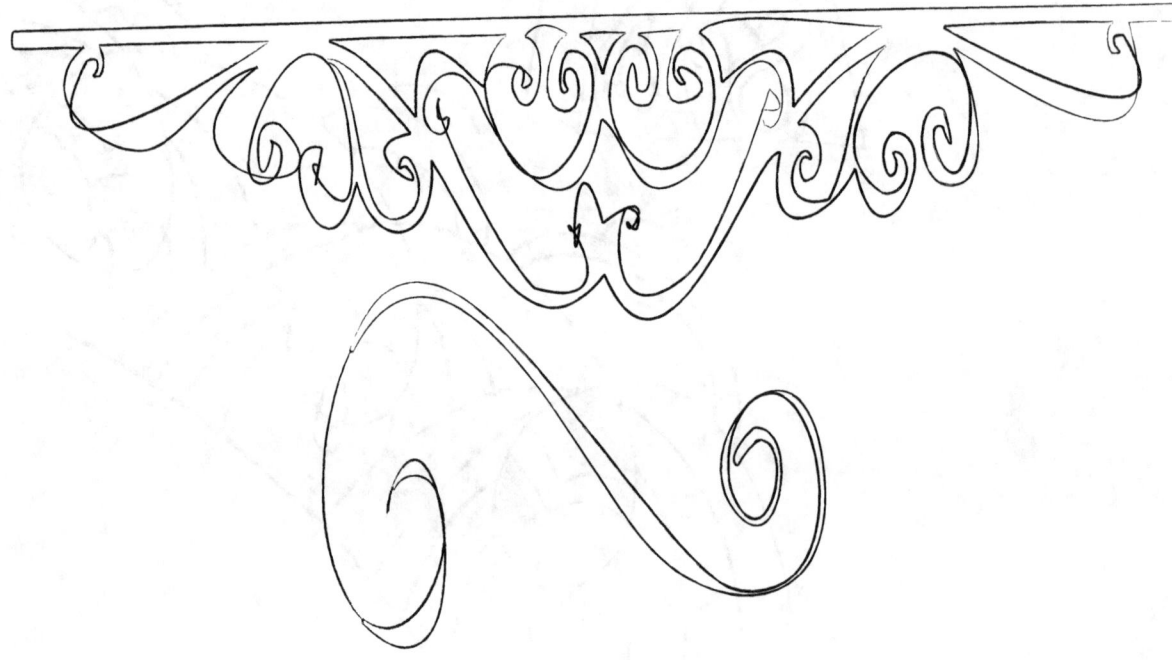

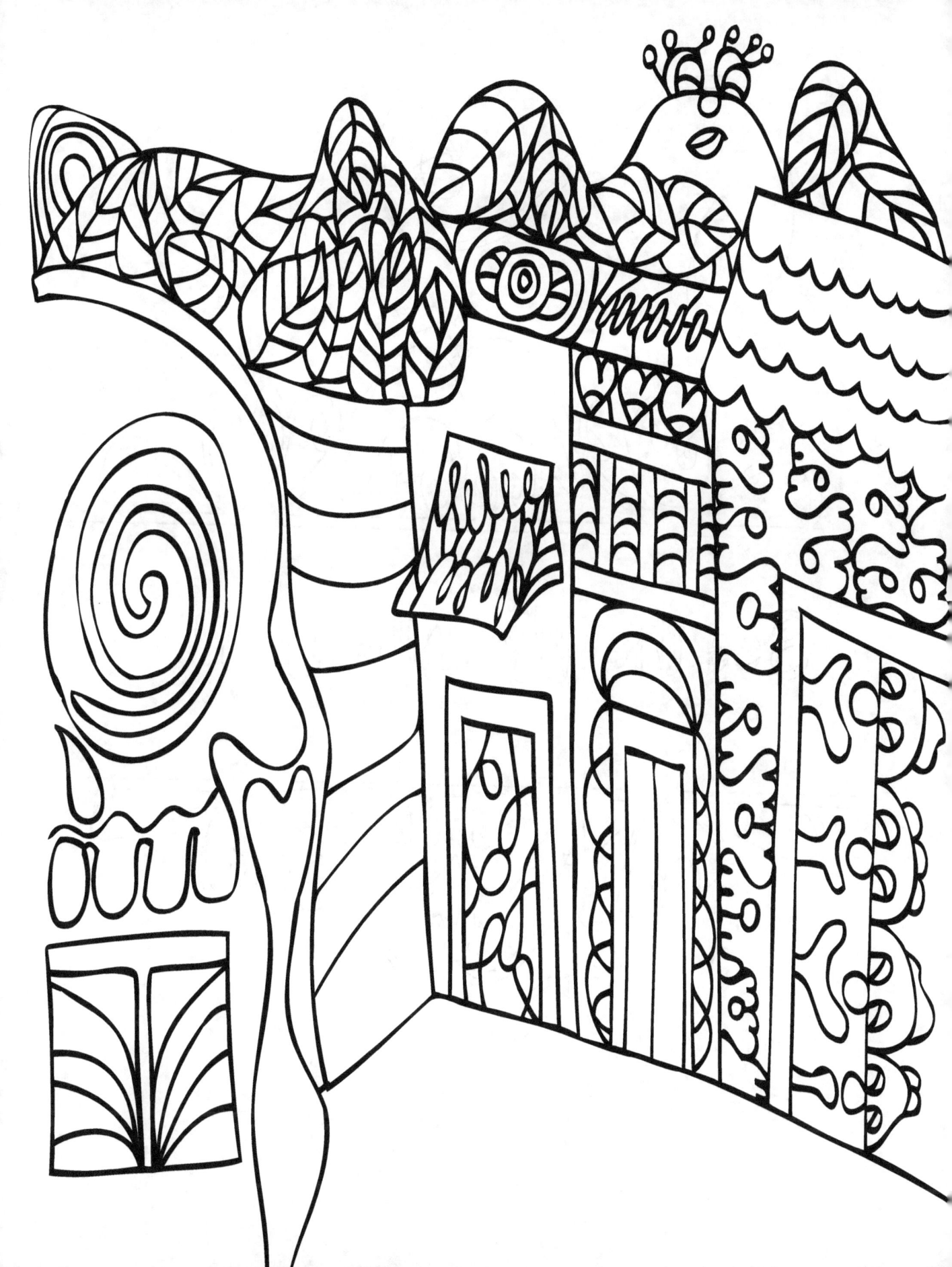

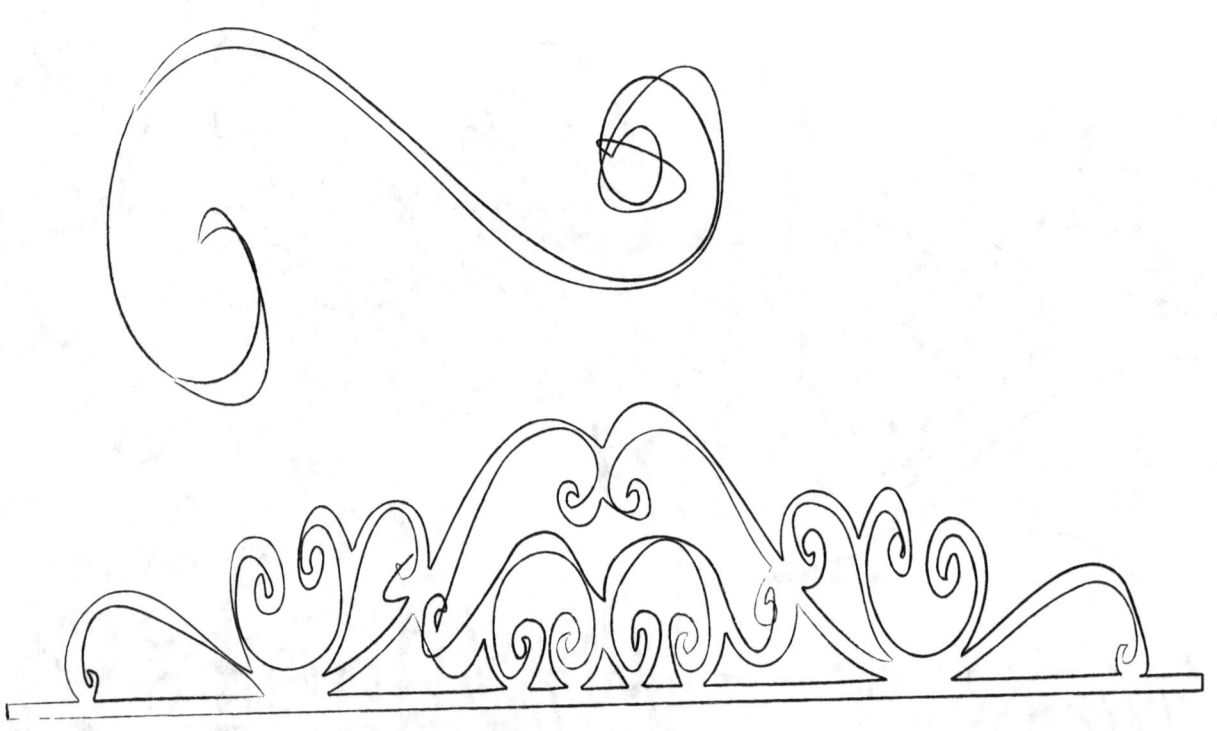

See the tity mile by mile

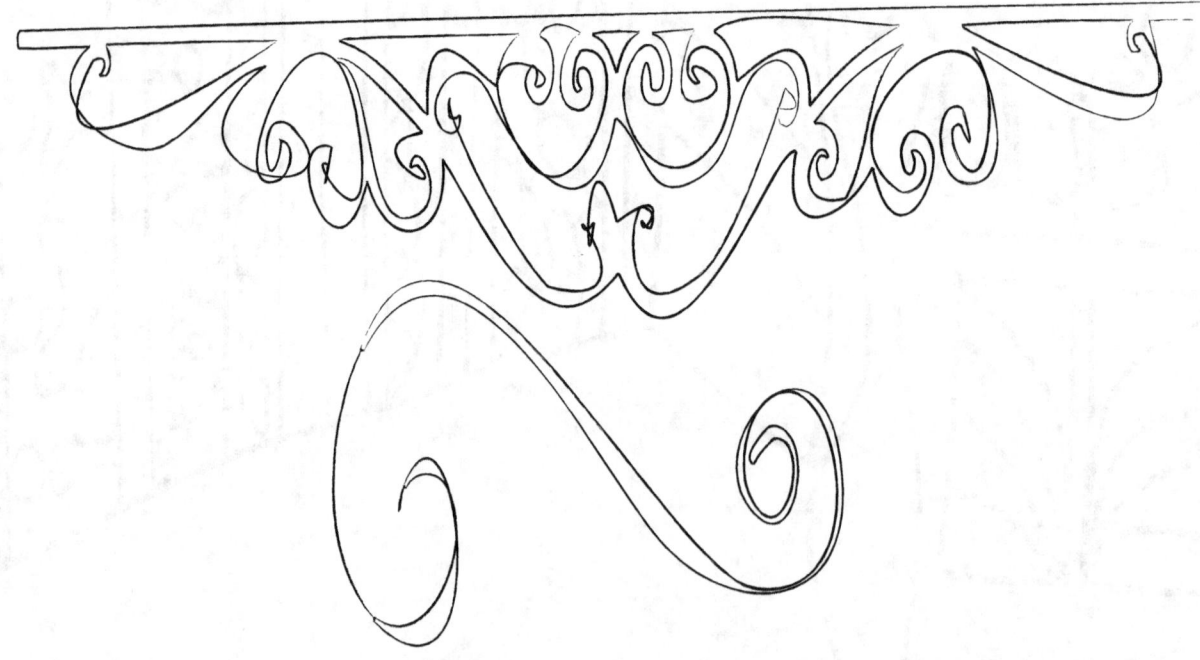

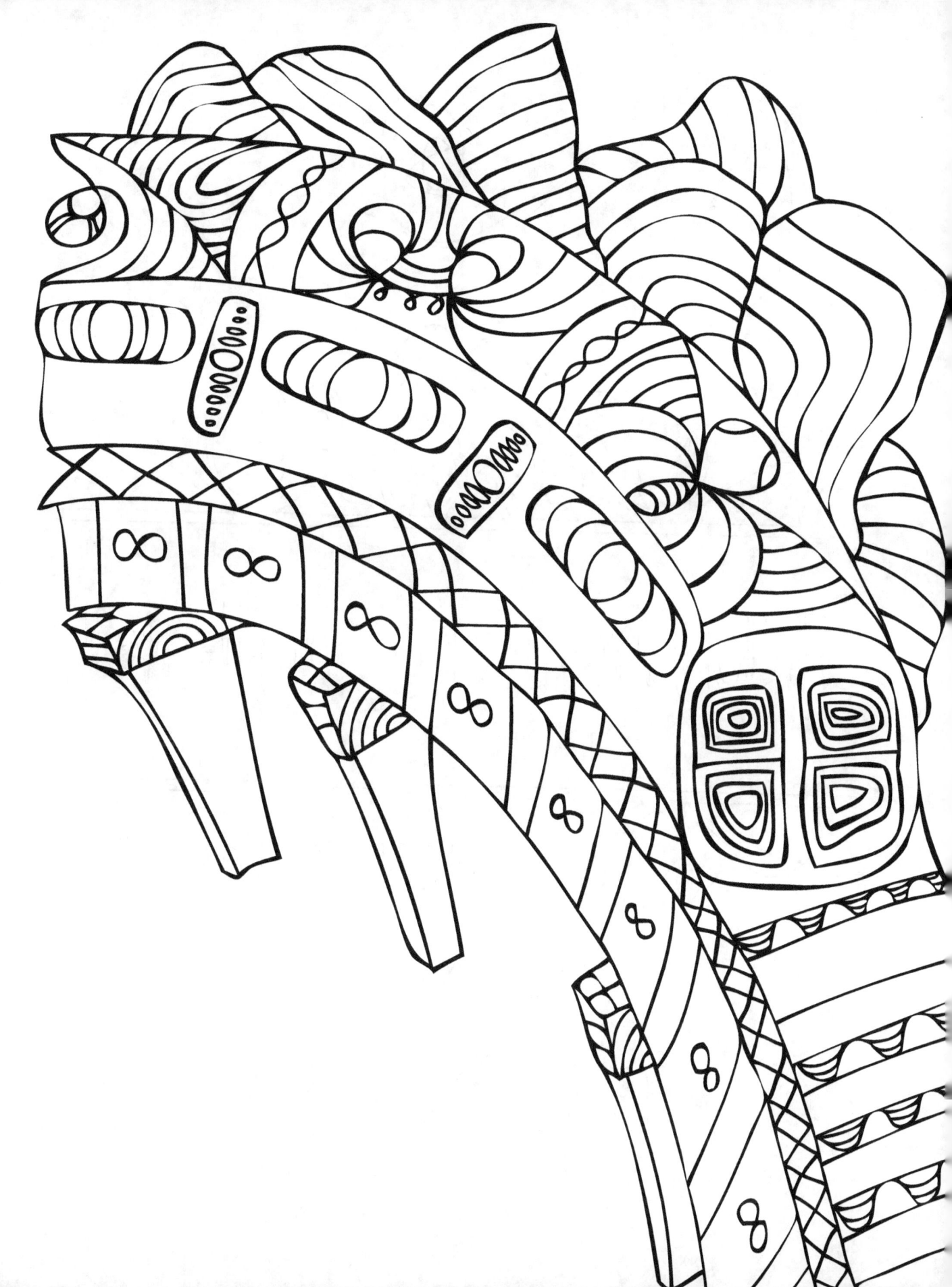

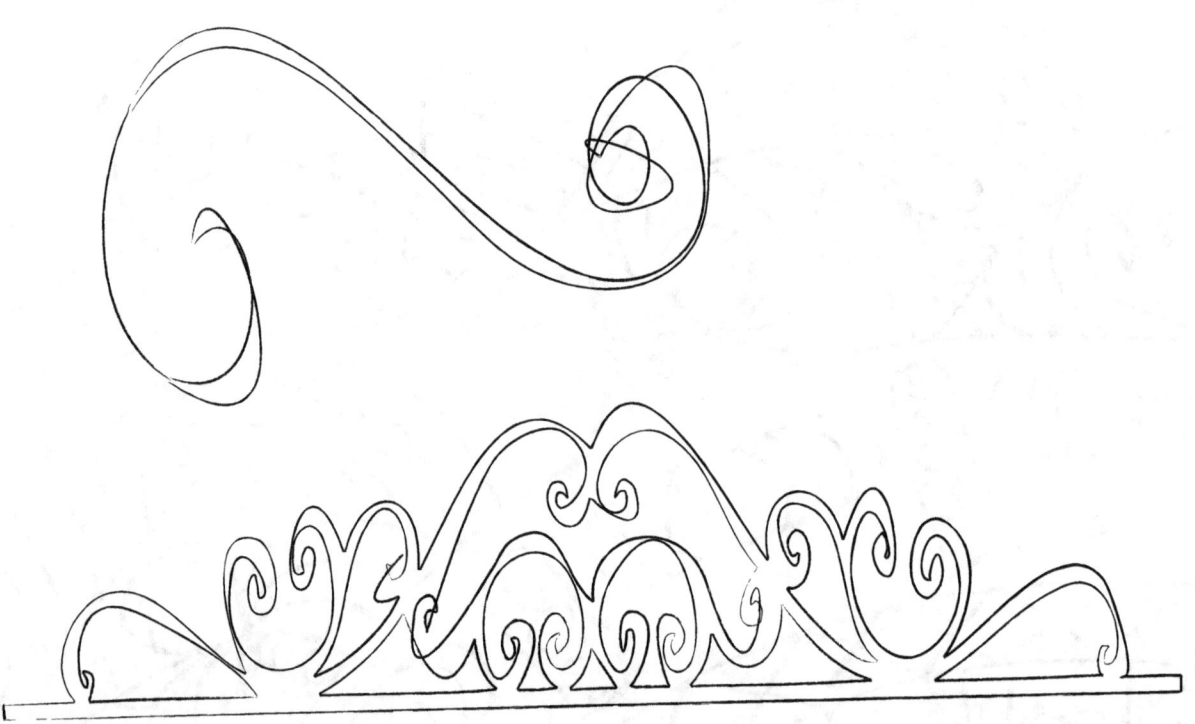

History interred but not silented

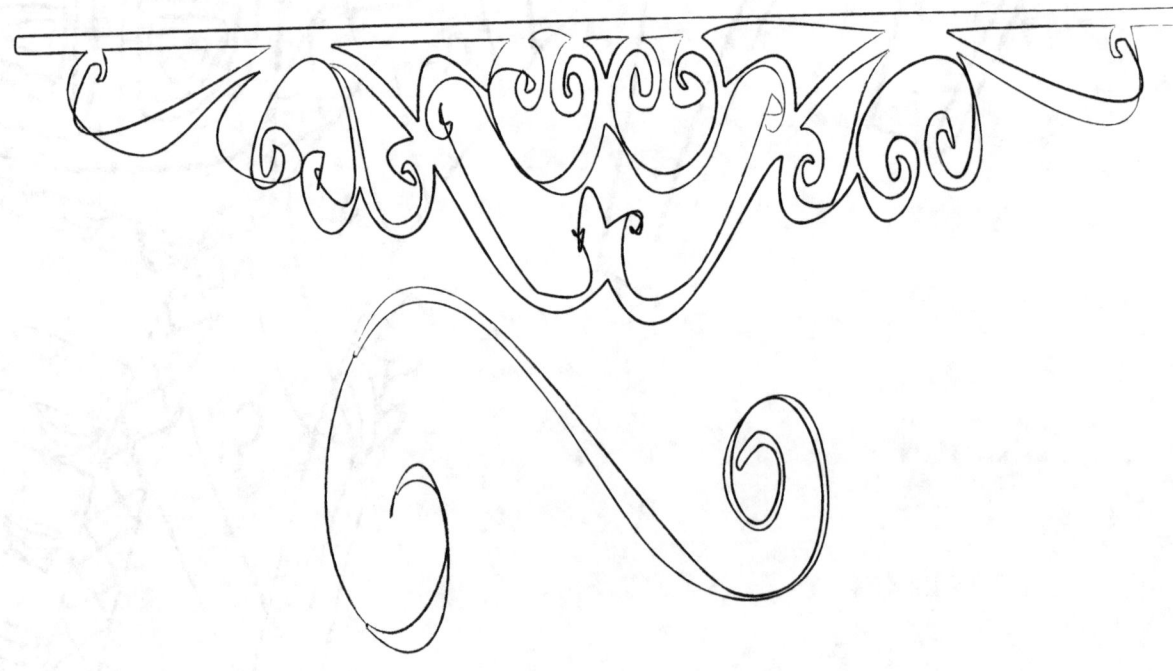

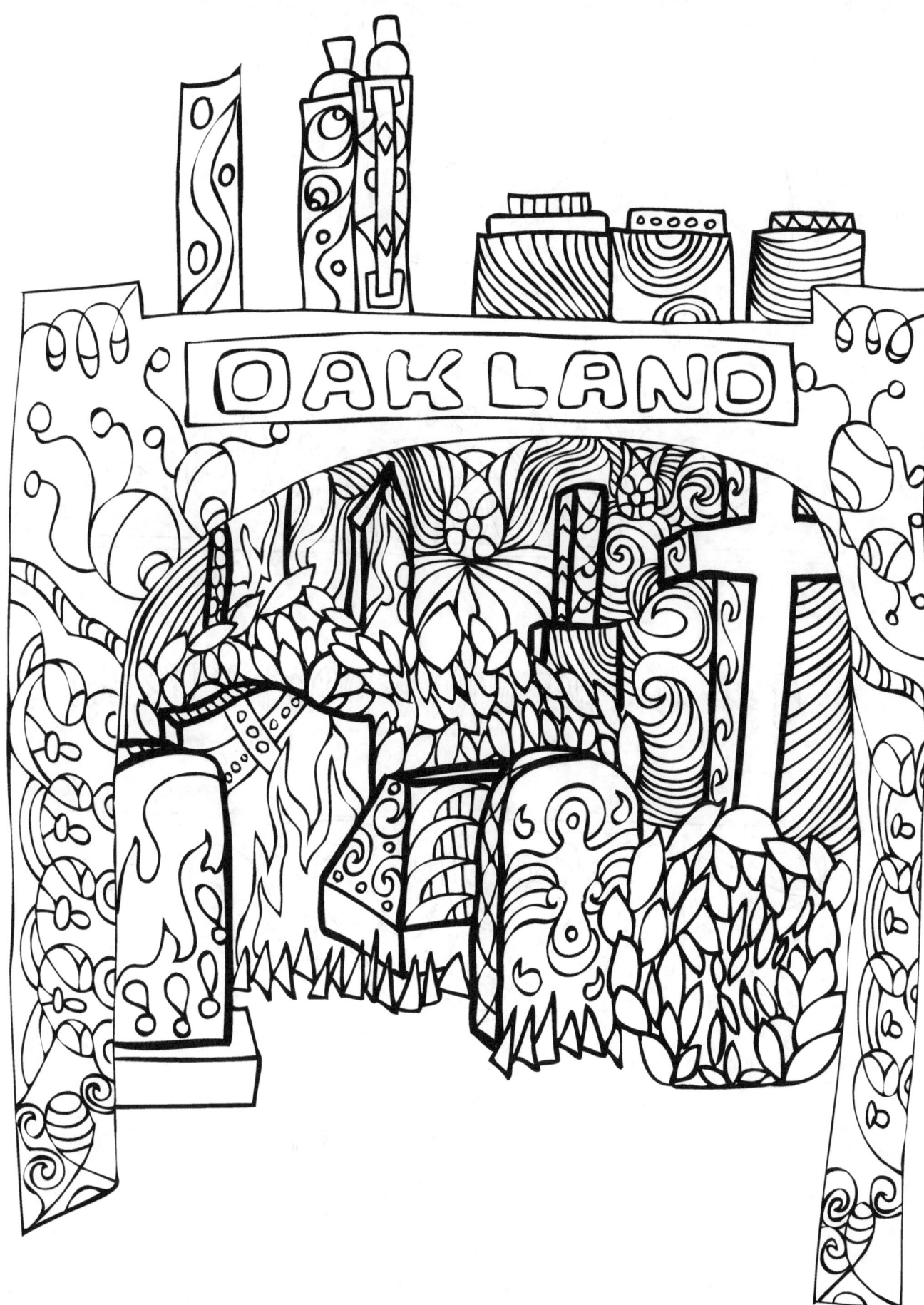

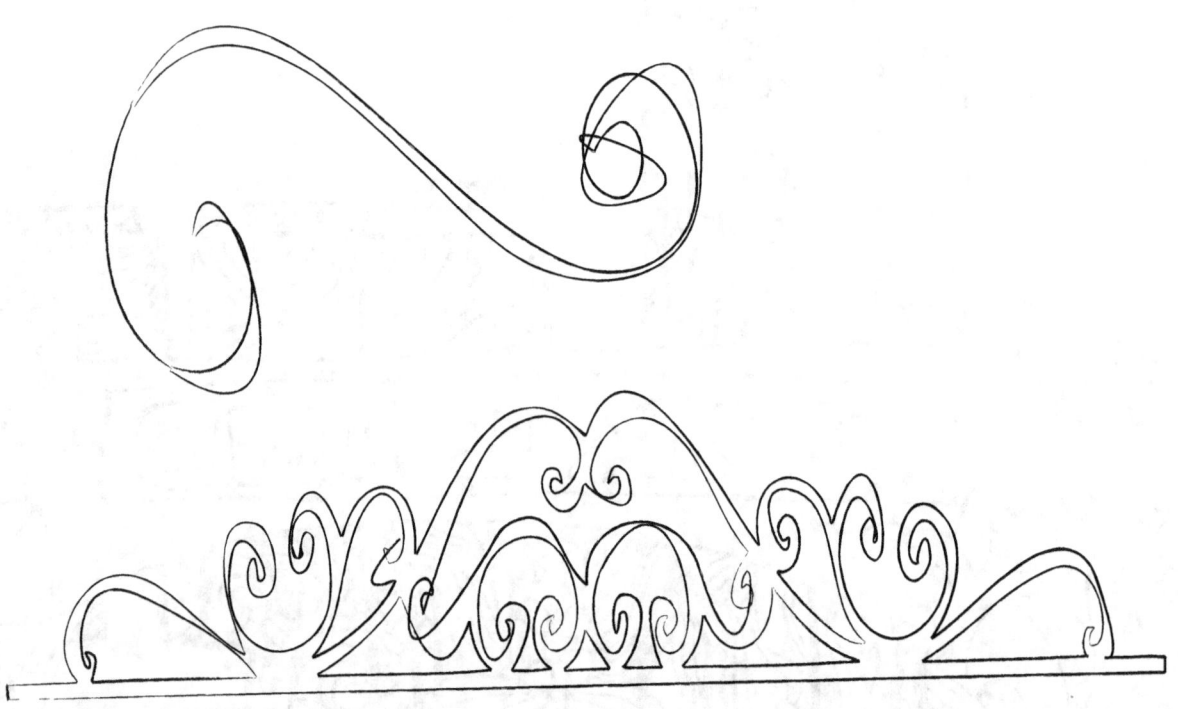

Georgia tales with Roman entrante

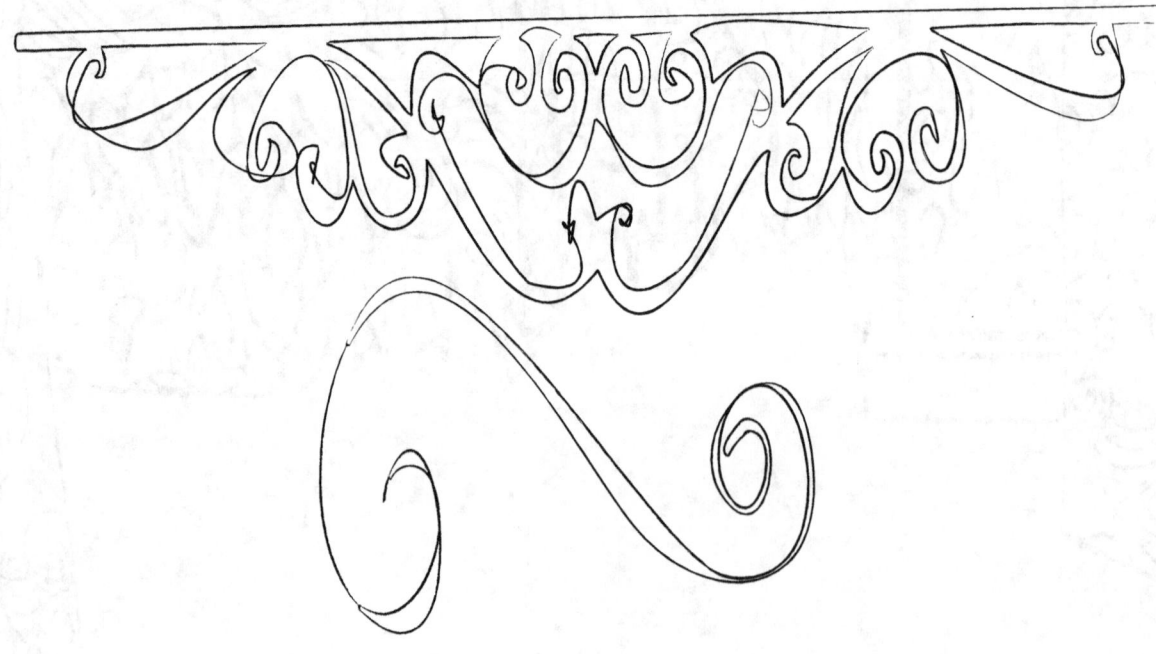

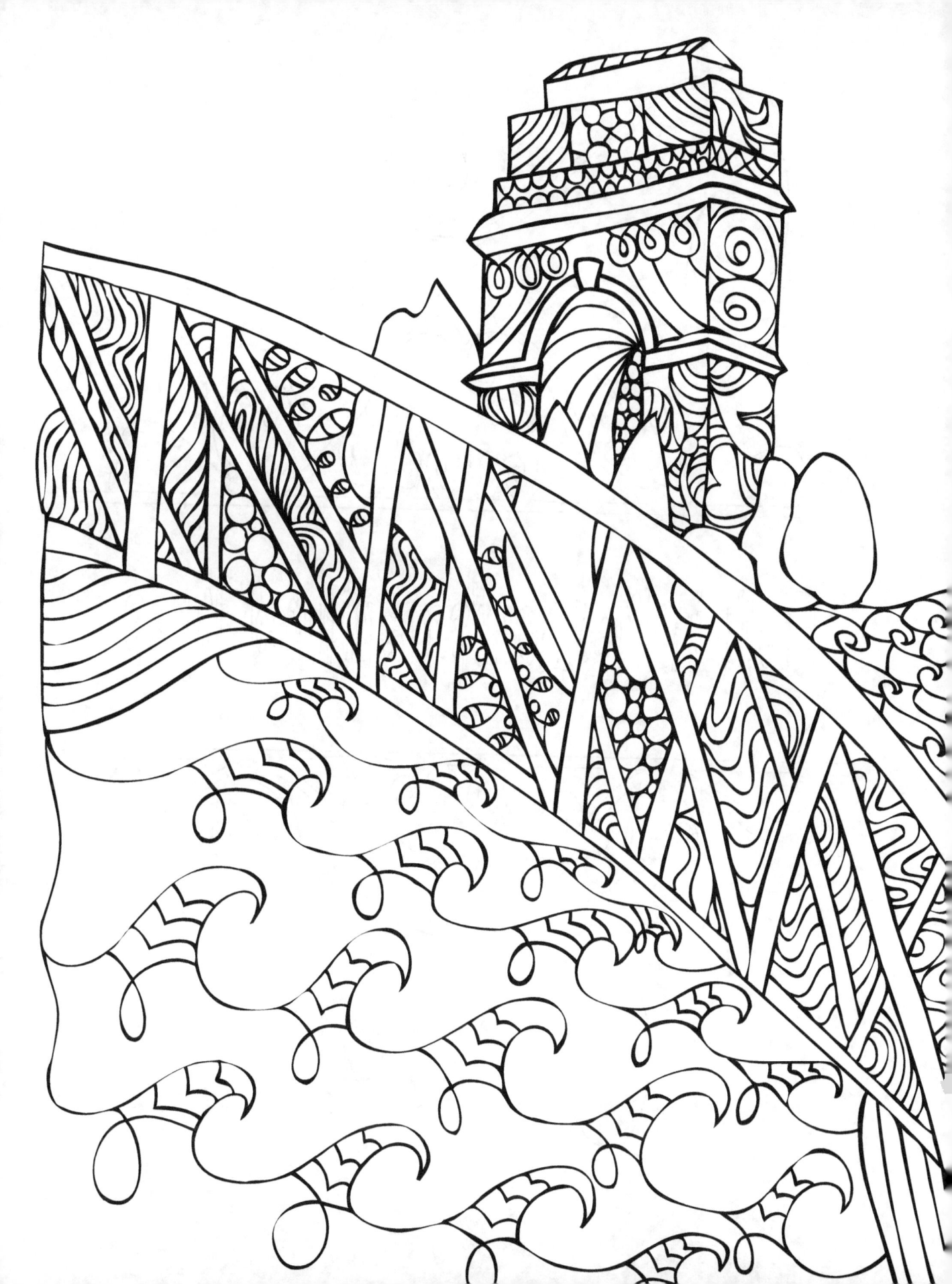

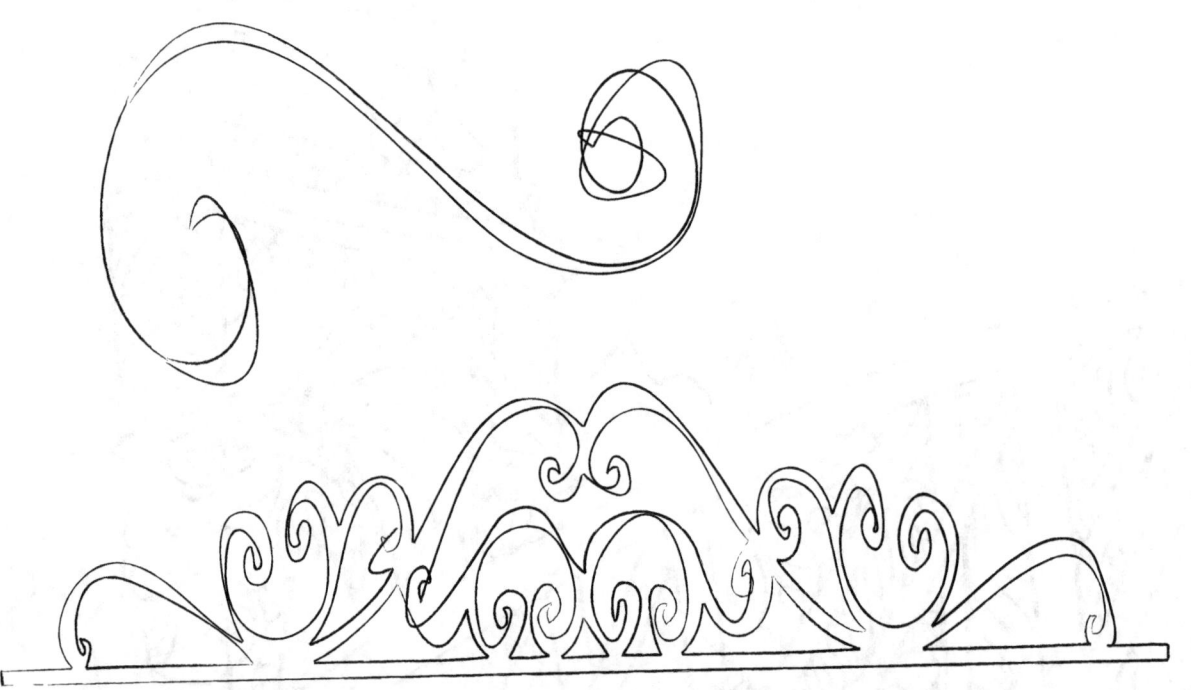

Frolic in Piedmont's manicured lanes

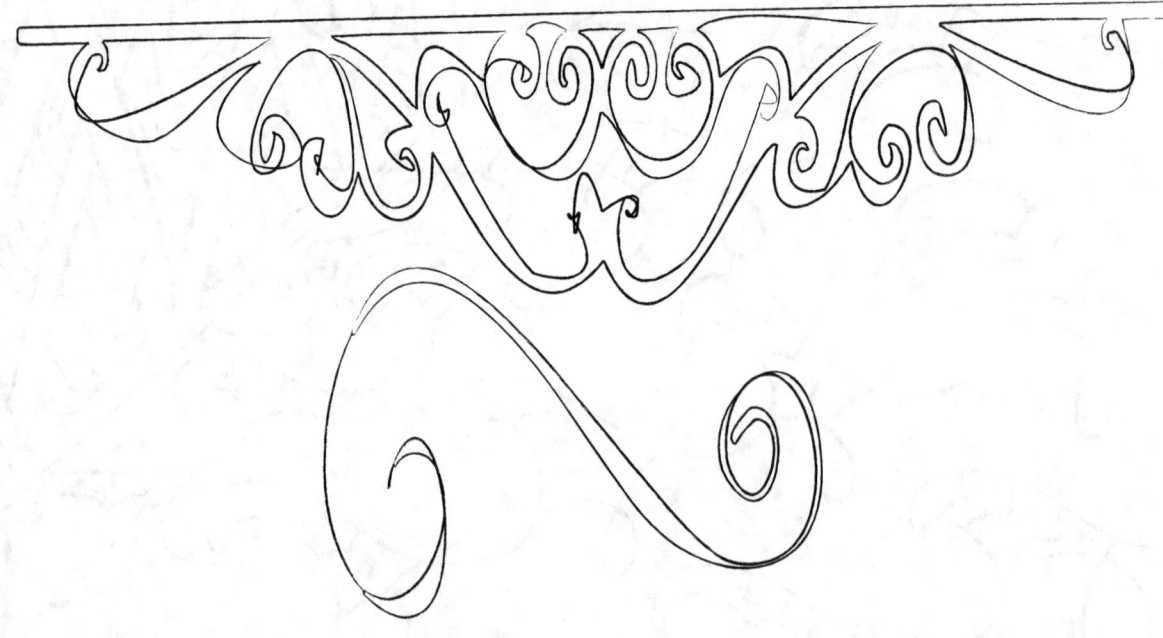

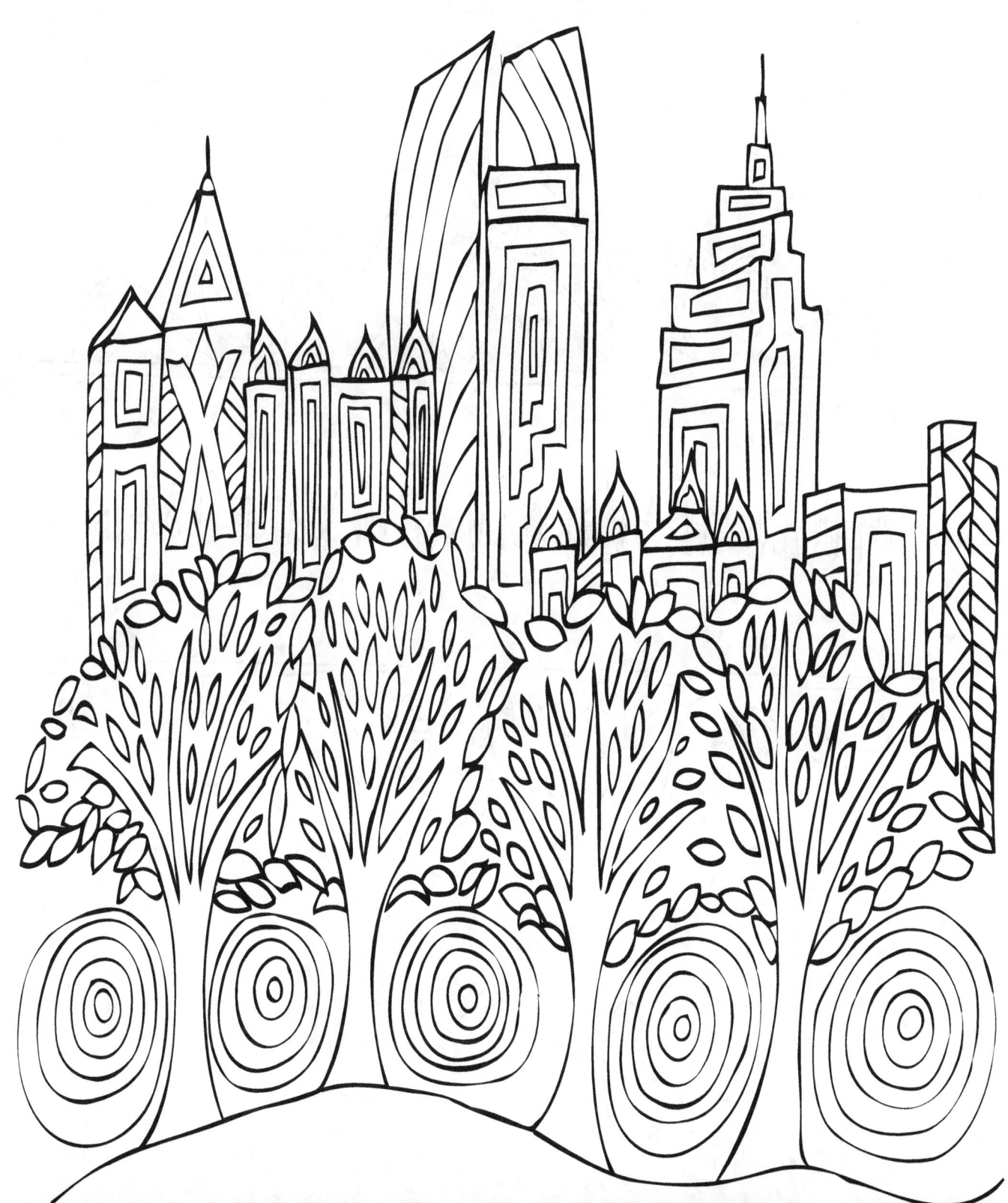

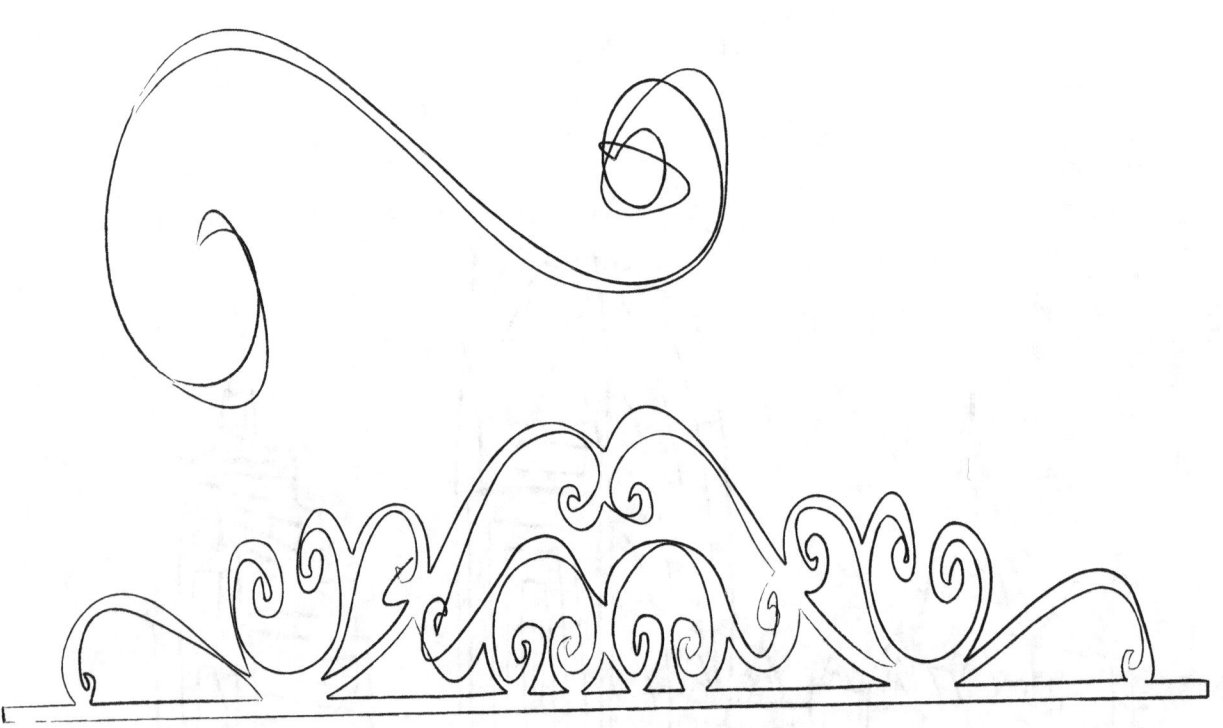

Industrial Westside rail yard trains

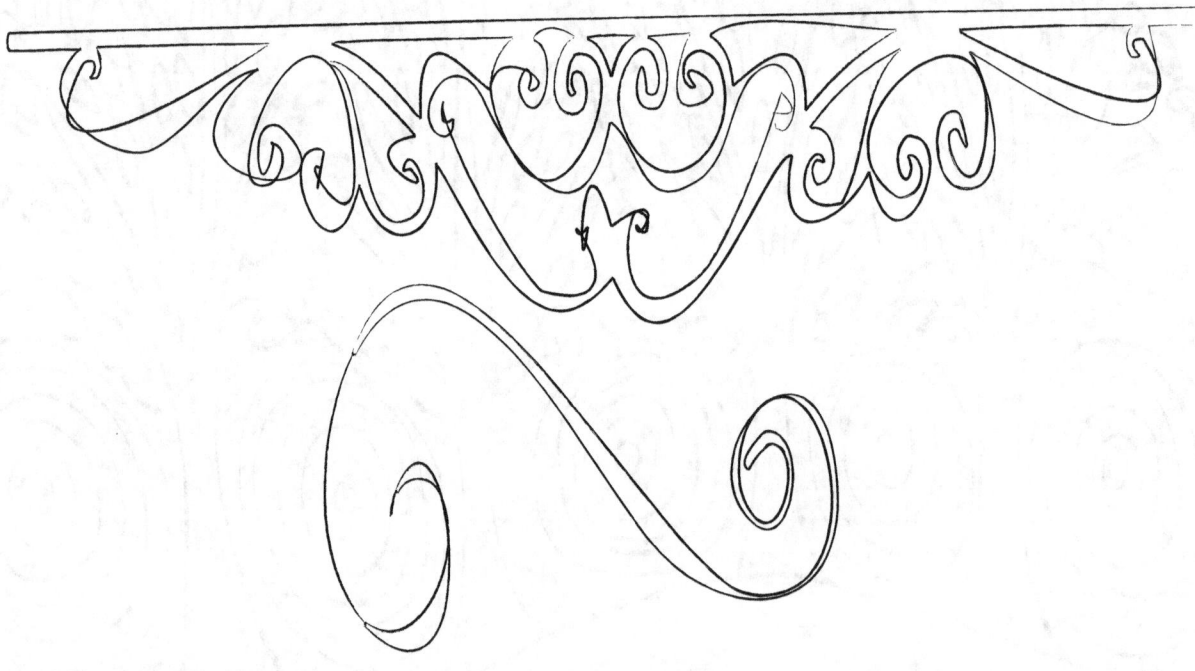

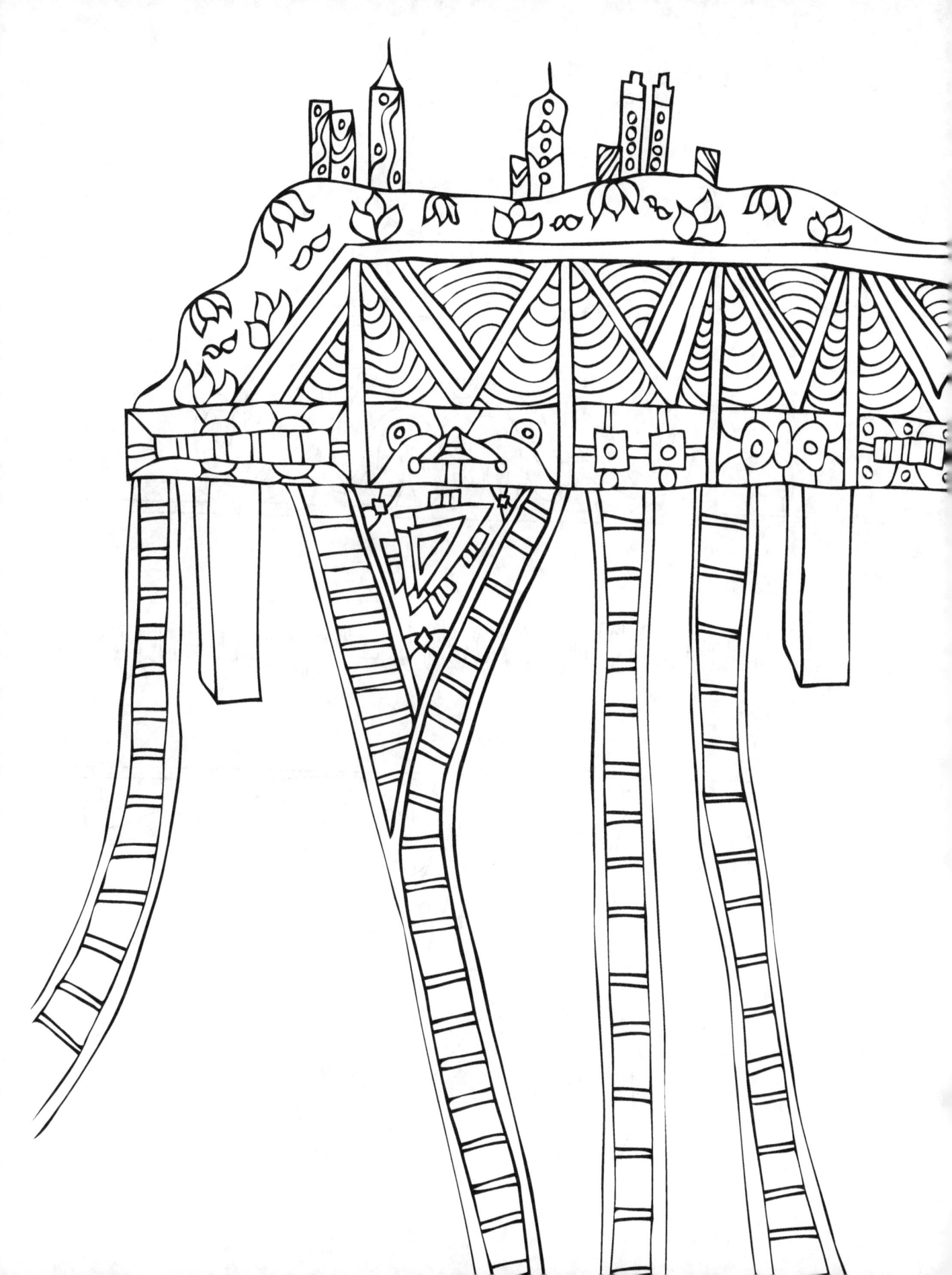

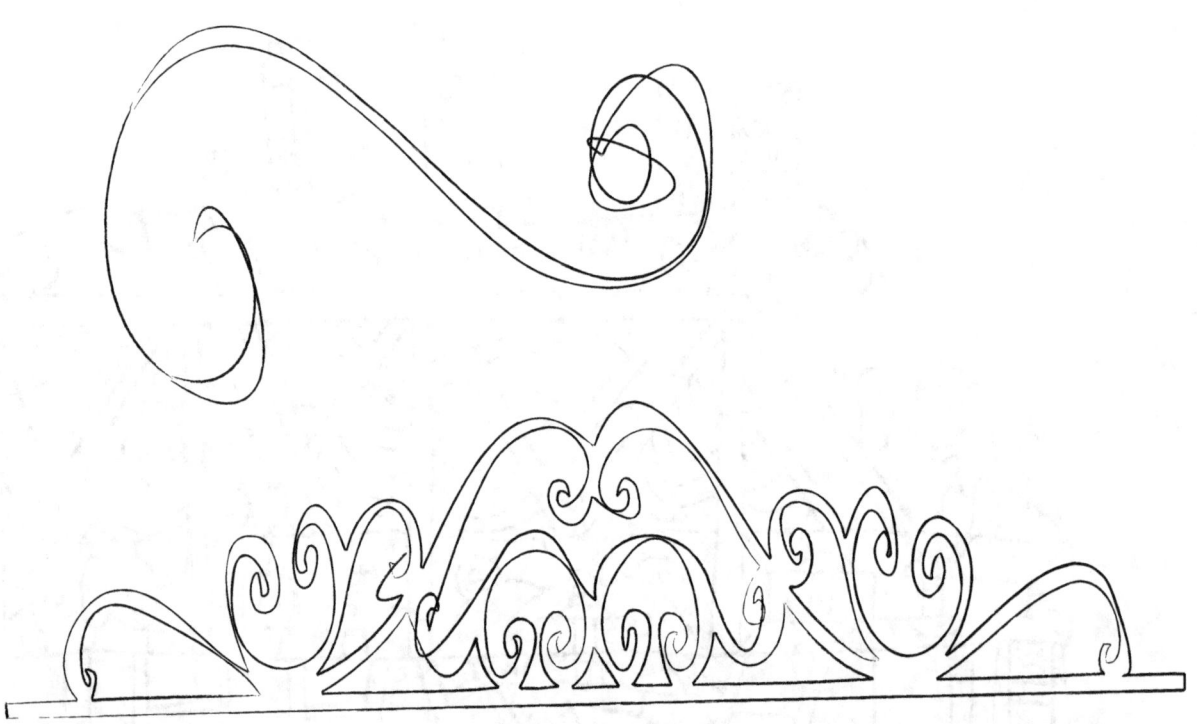

Buildings built around Egyptian things

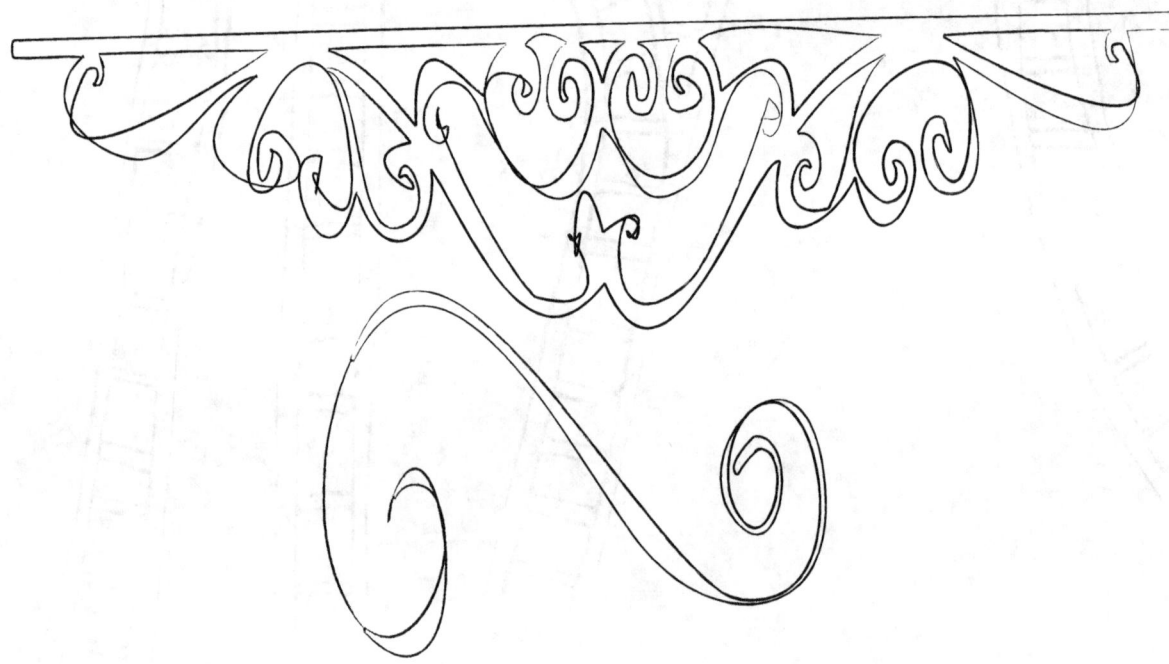

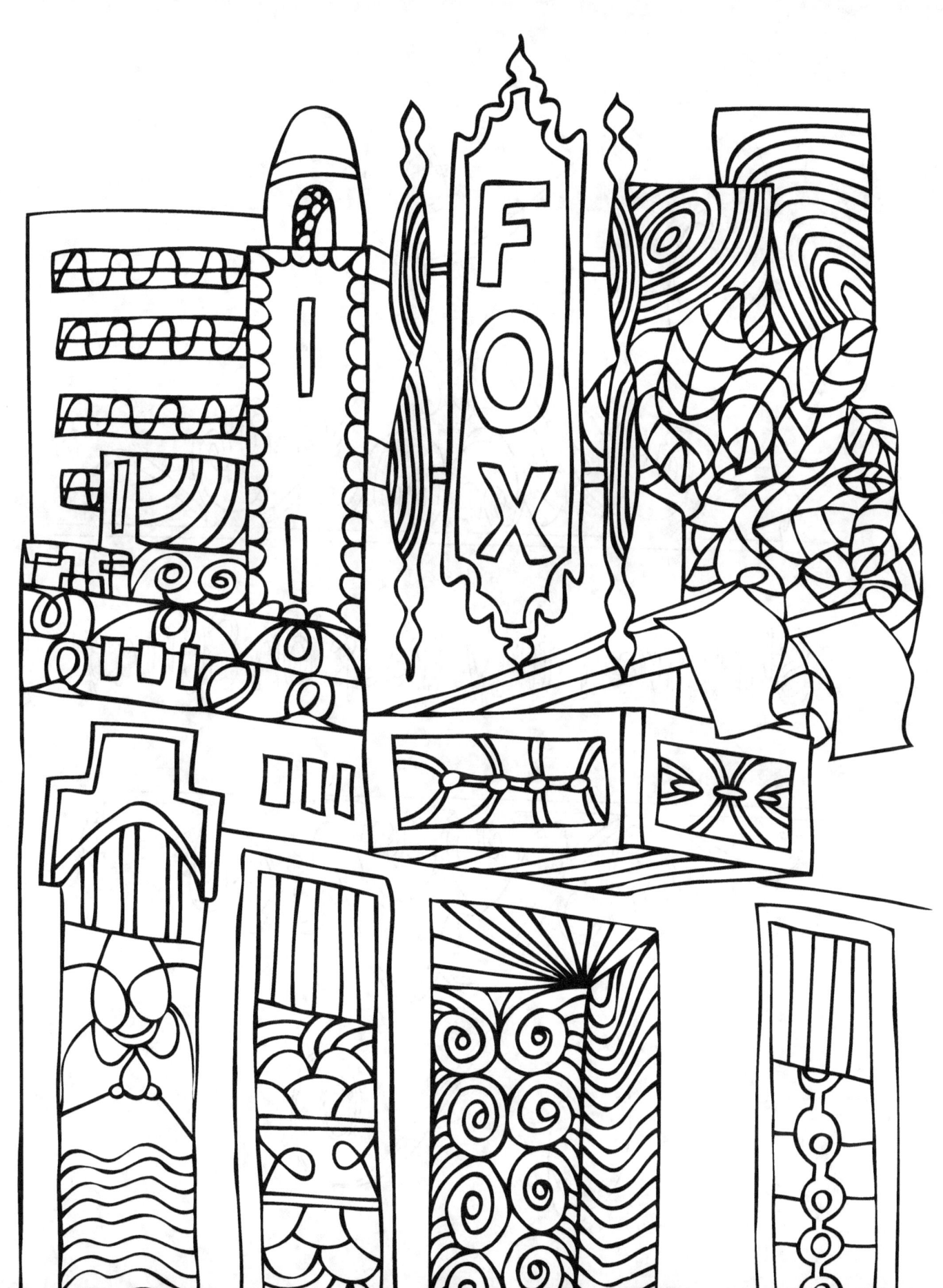

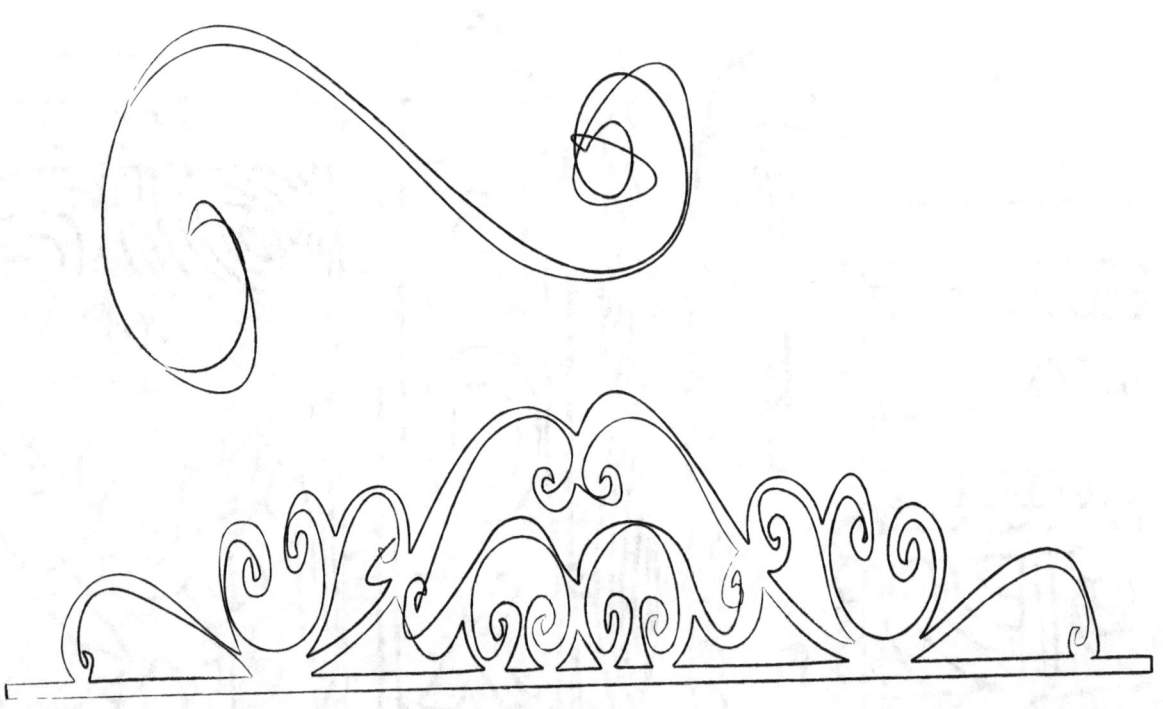

Shrunken tiny trees on Spring

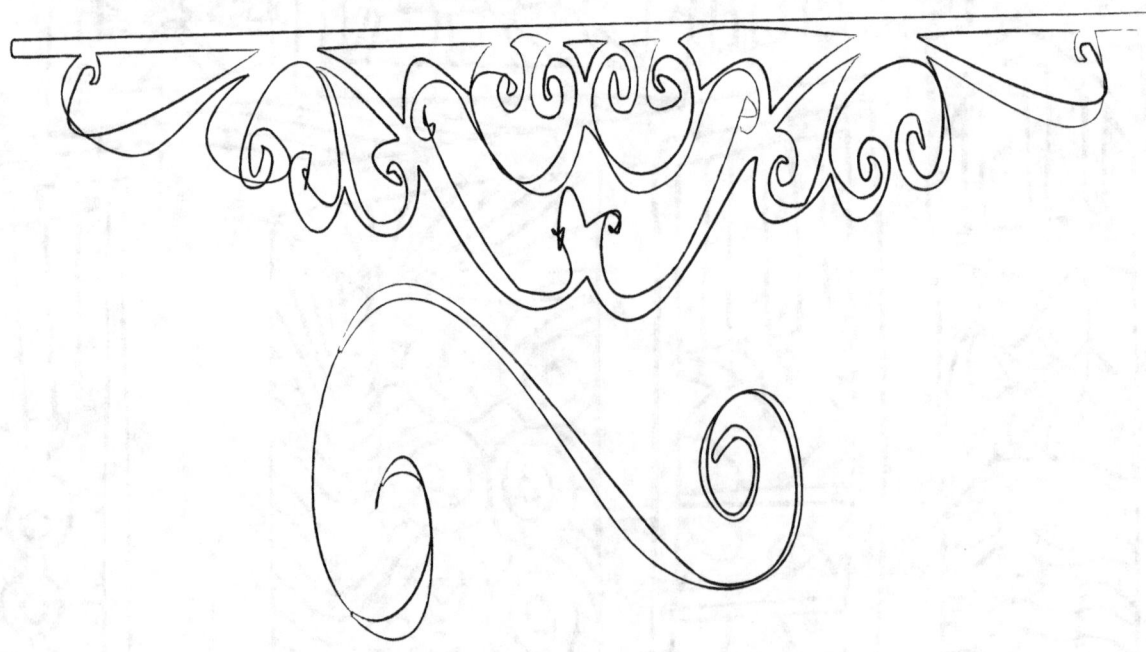

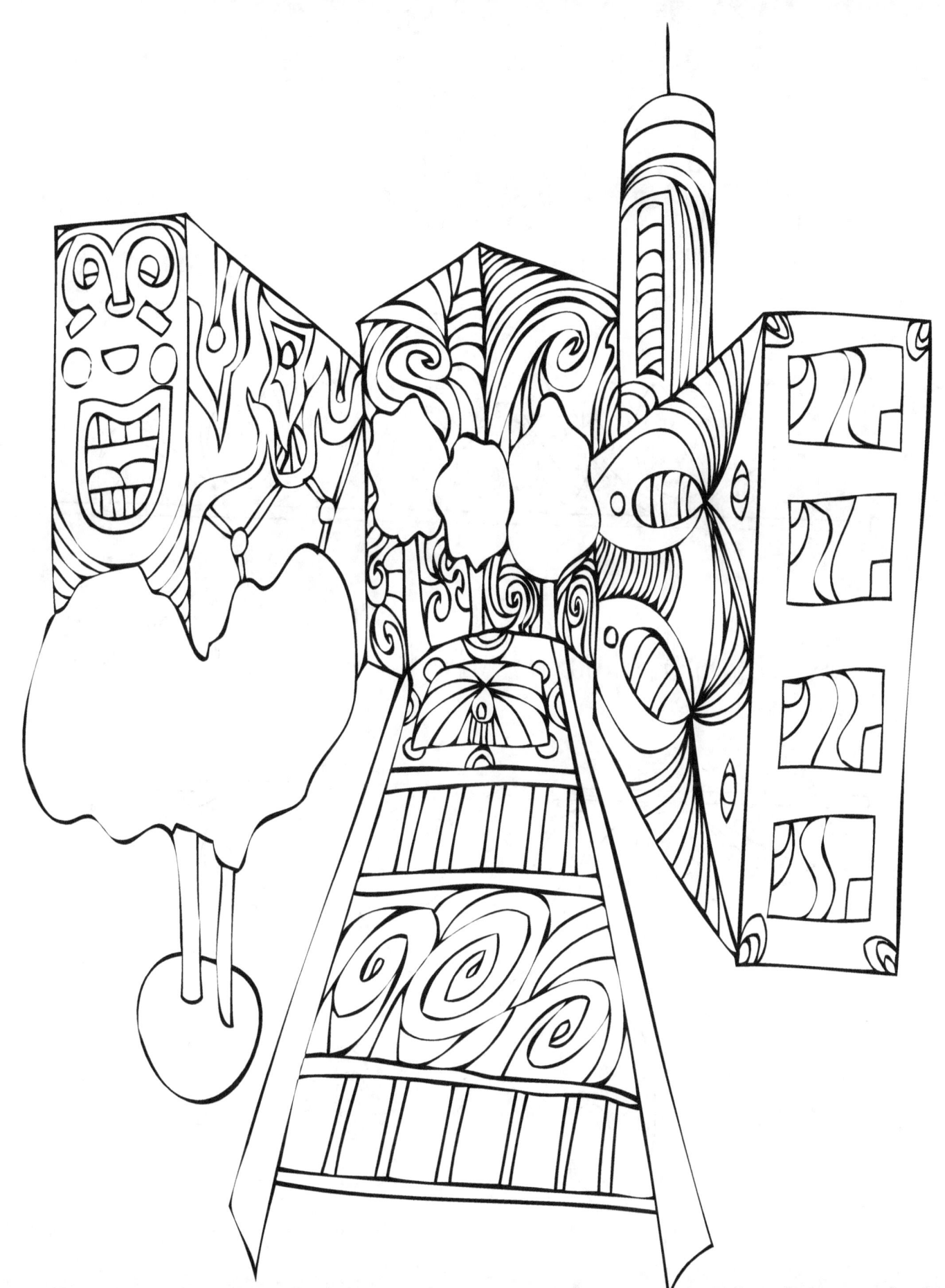

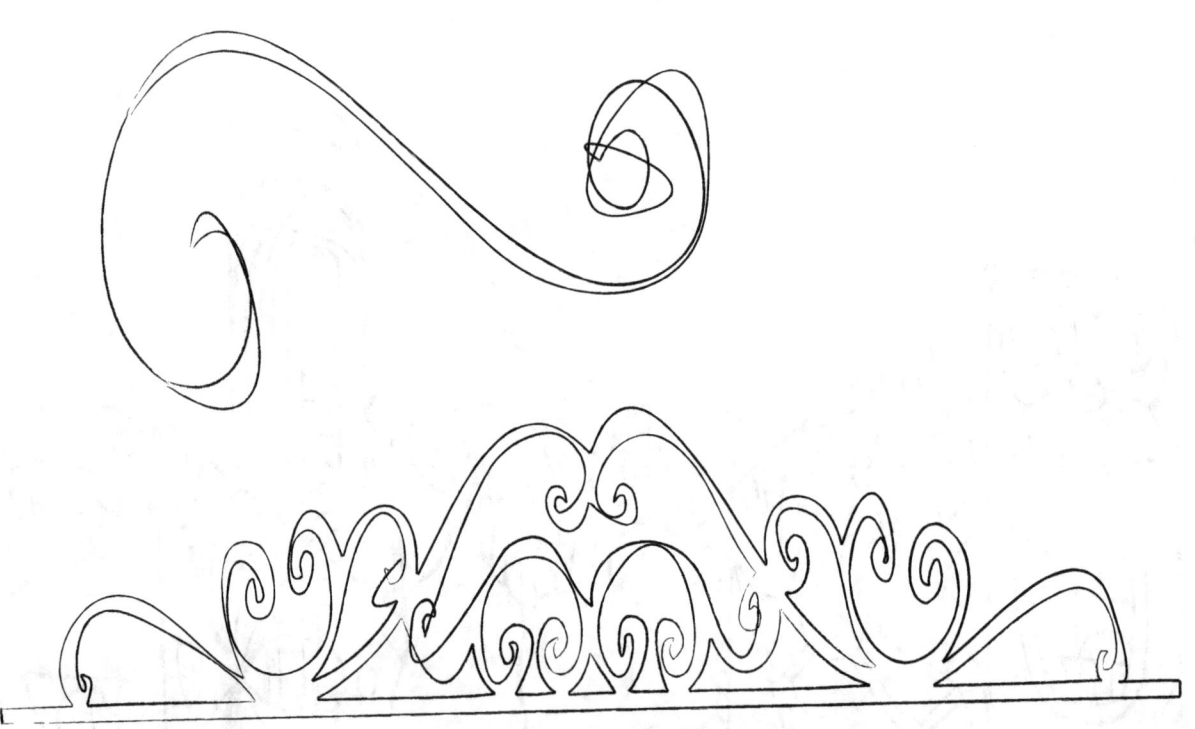

Remember the summer the world watched from afar

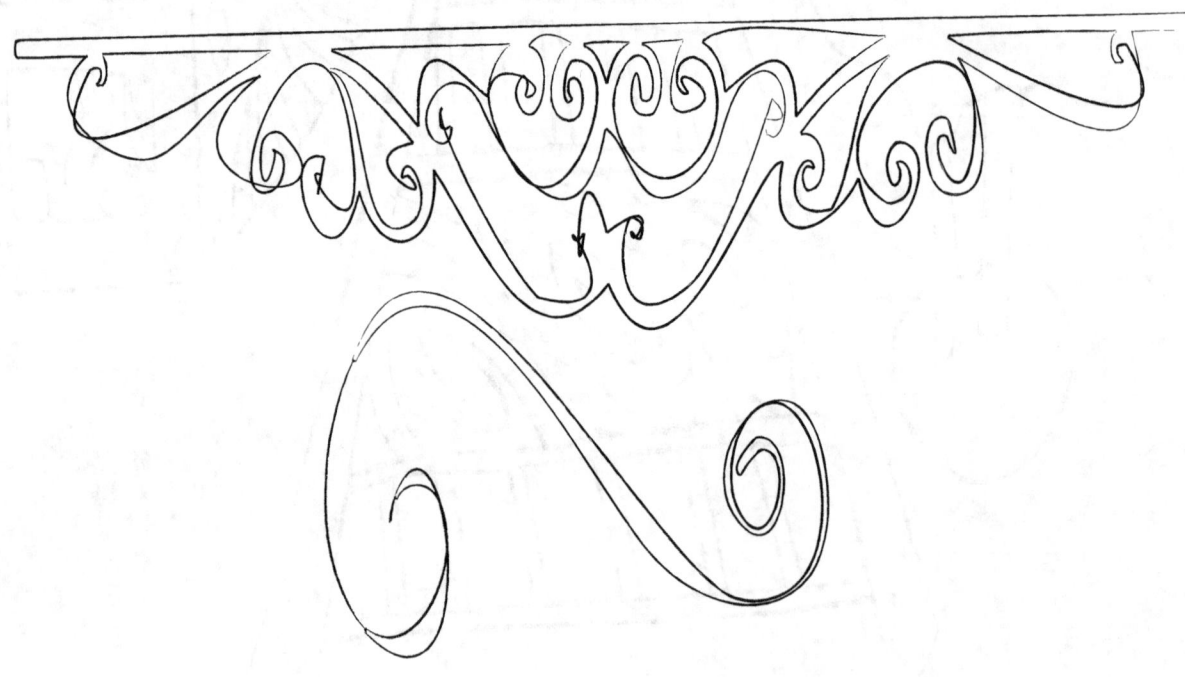

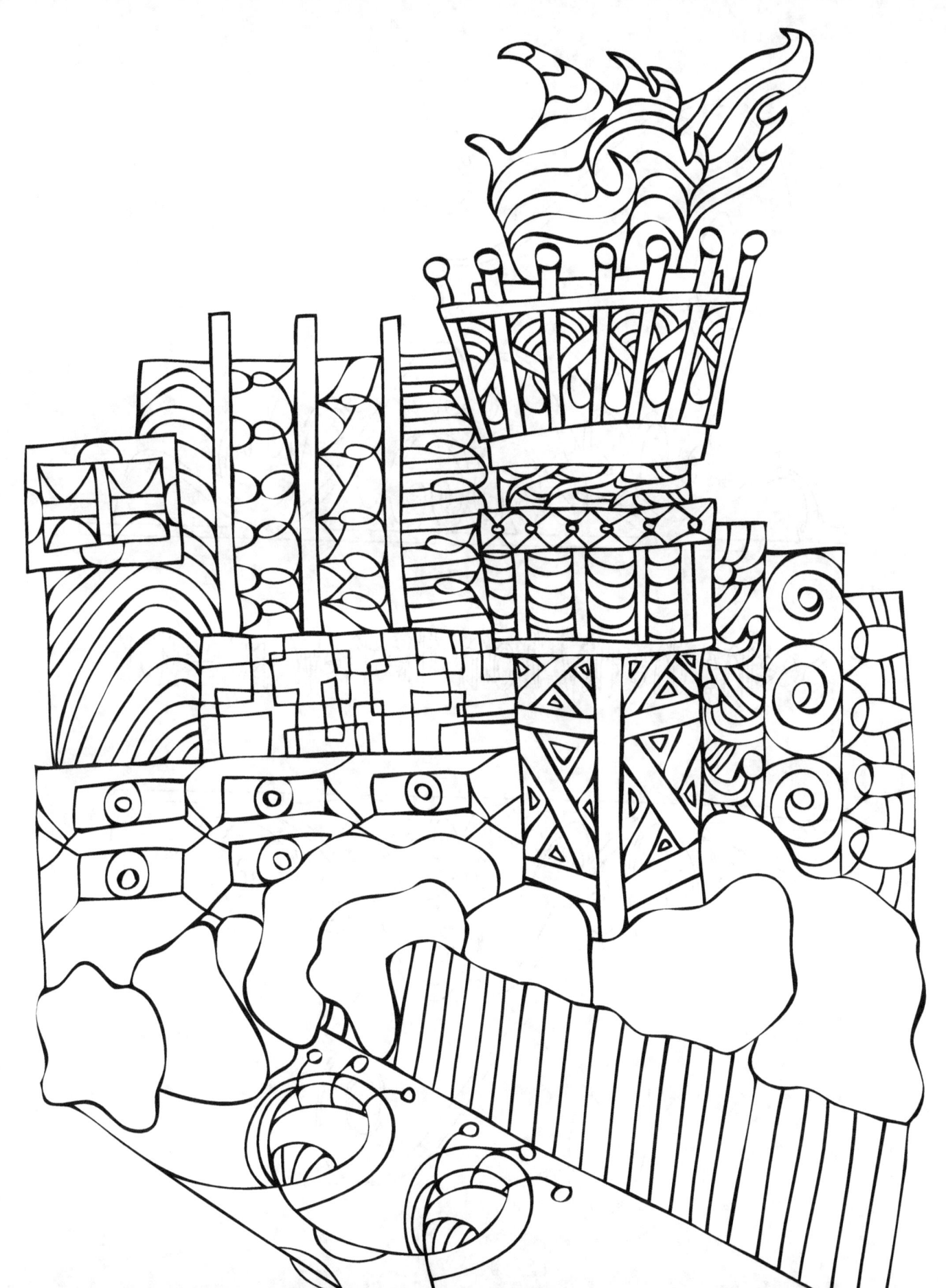

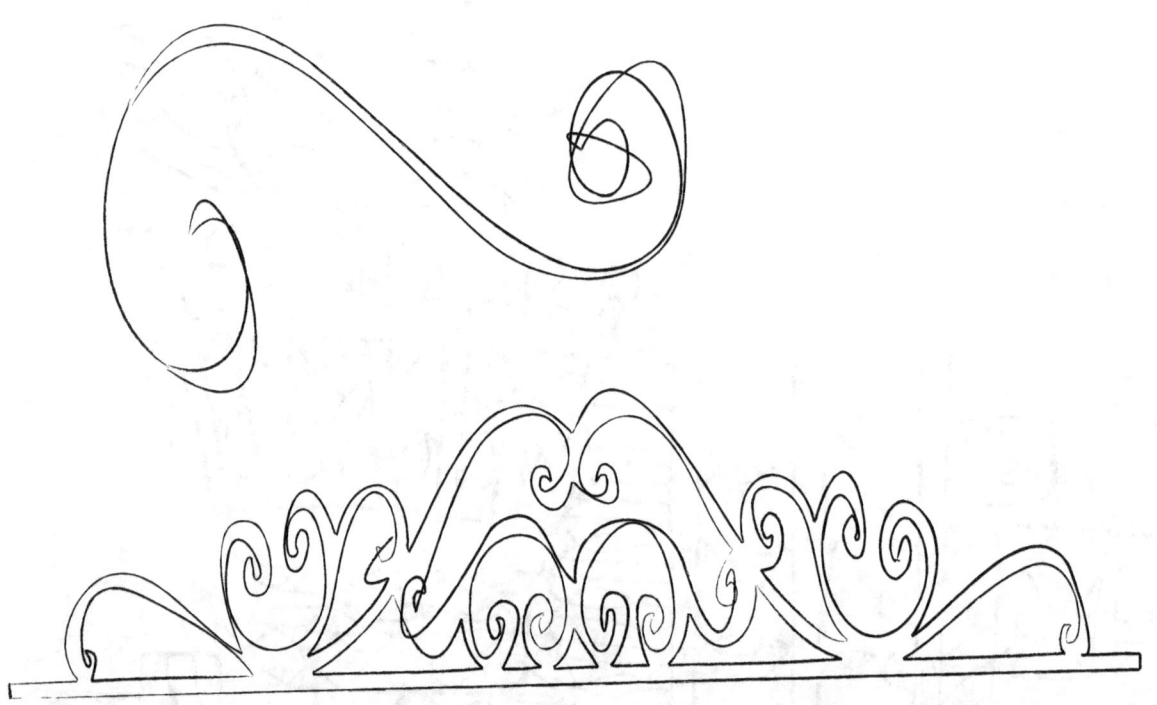

Seeing the city from the new streetcar

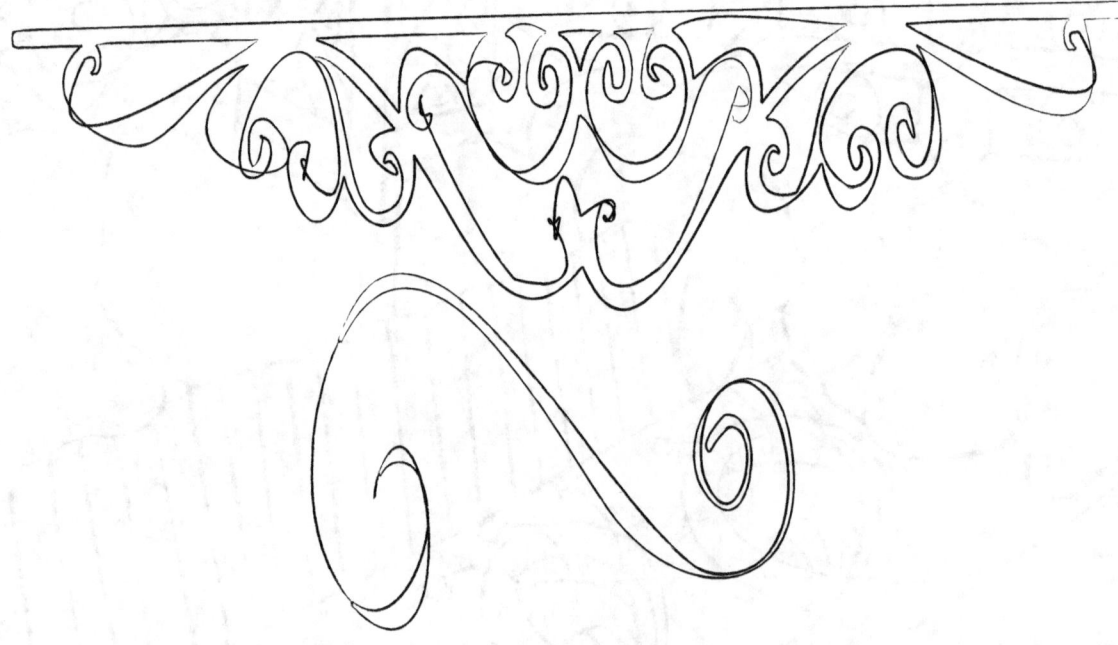

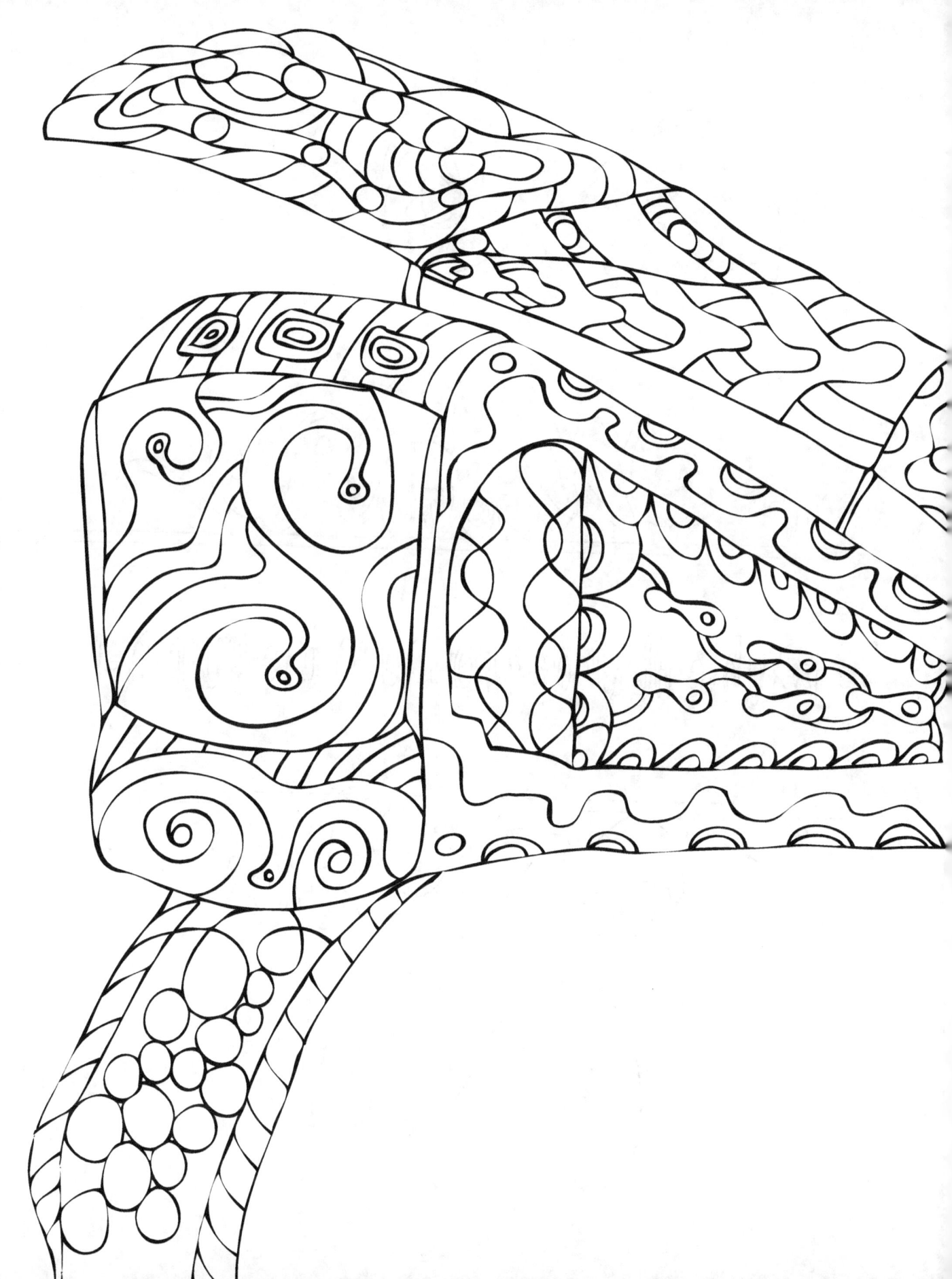

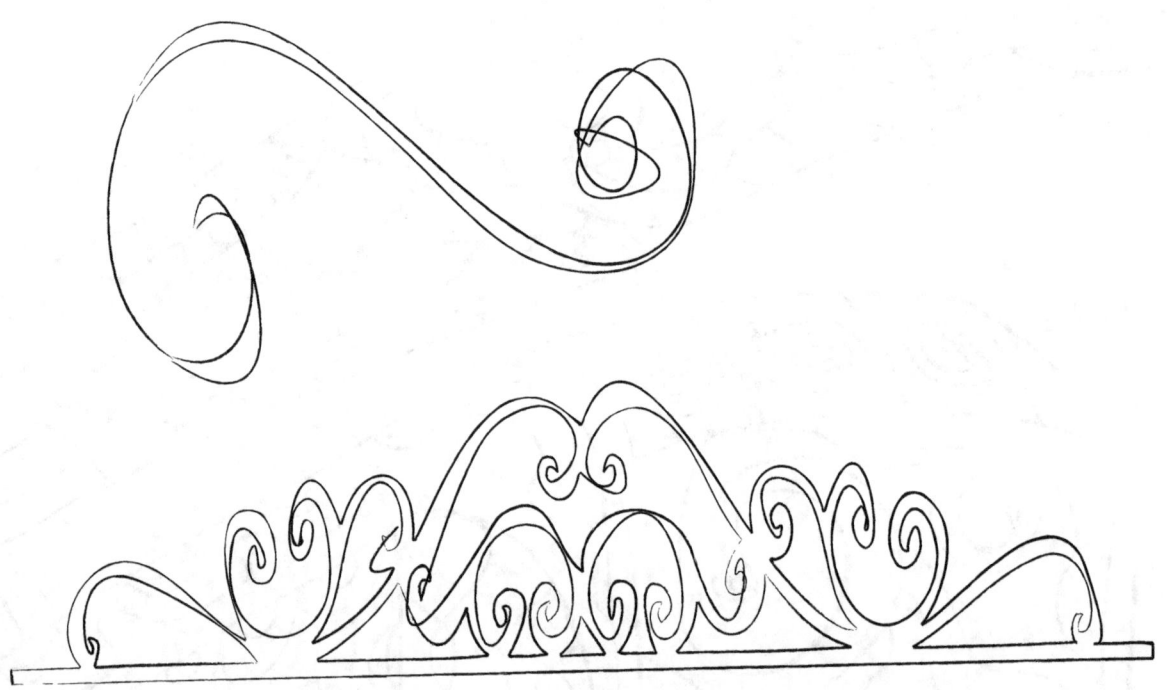

Bauble lit underground in the summer

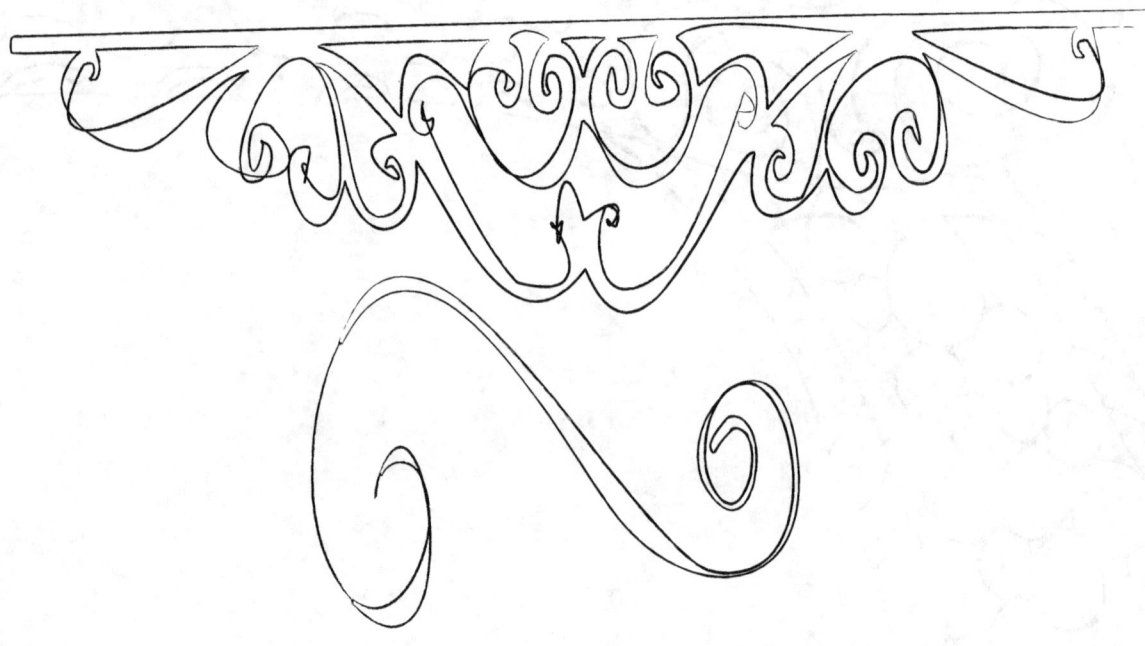

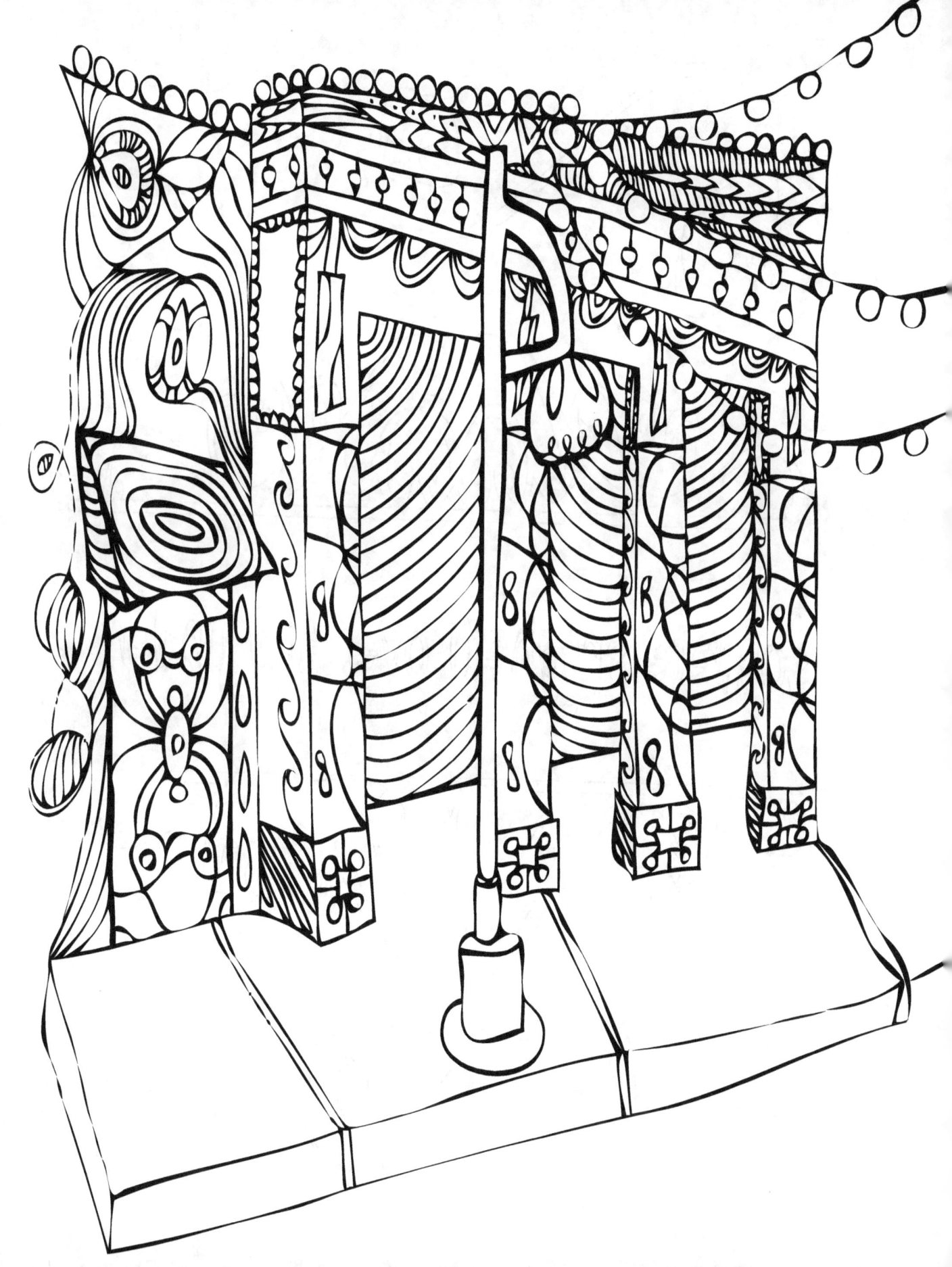

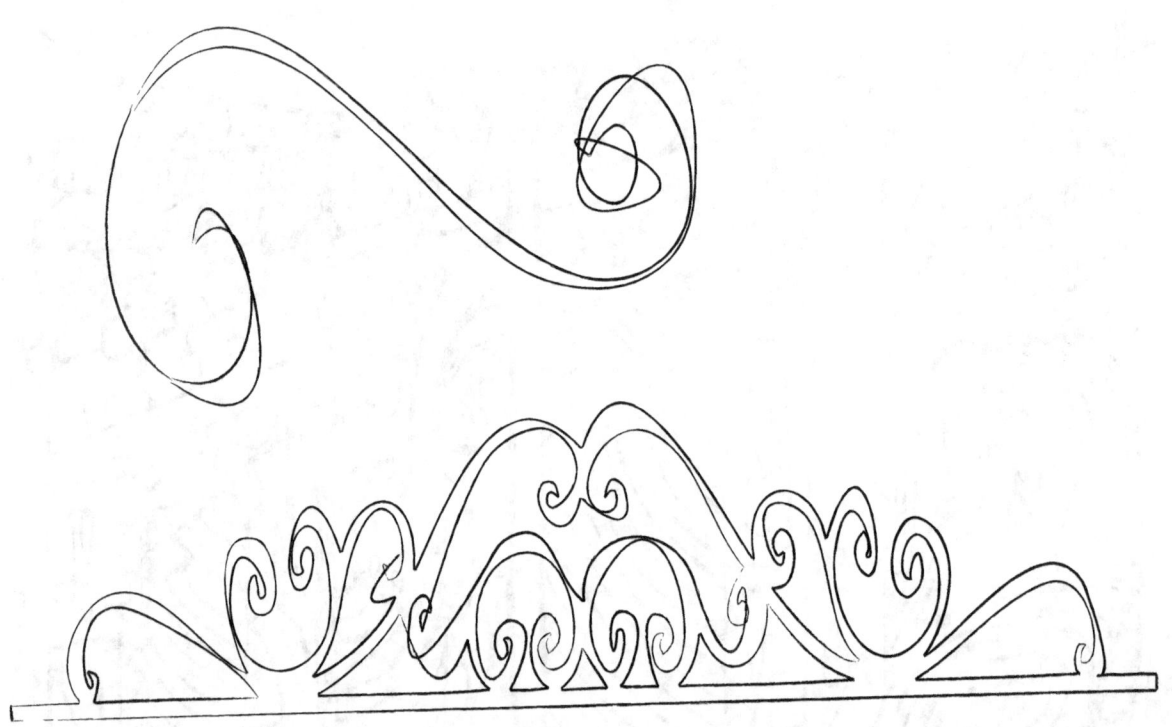

fontrete spaghetti over and under

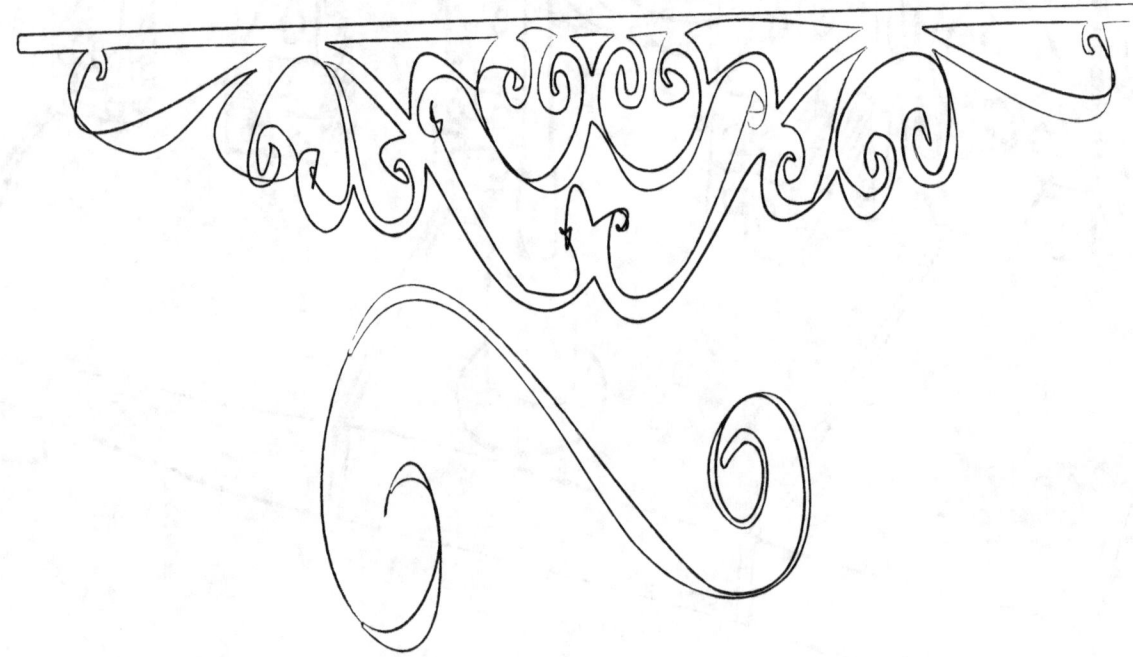

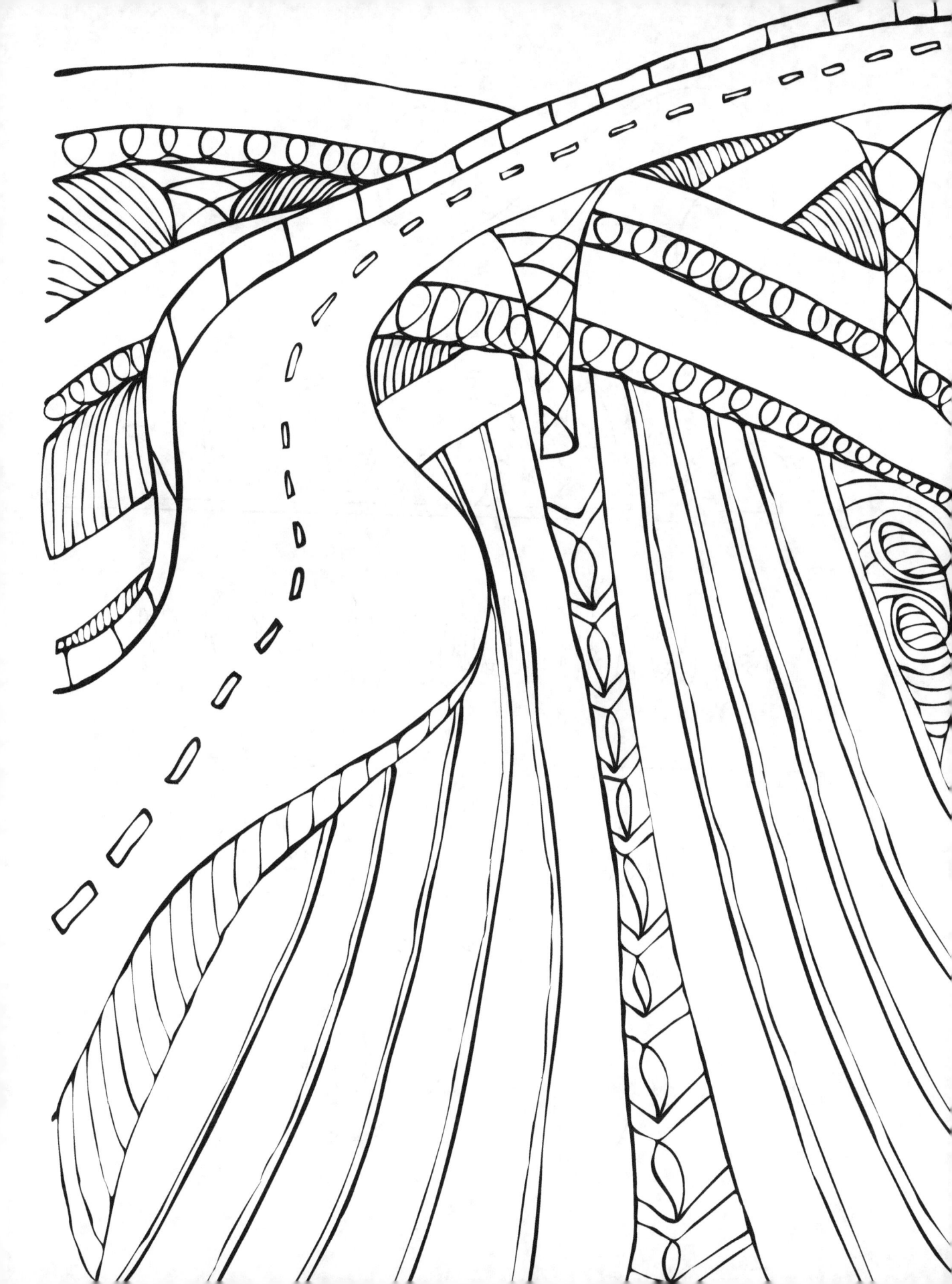

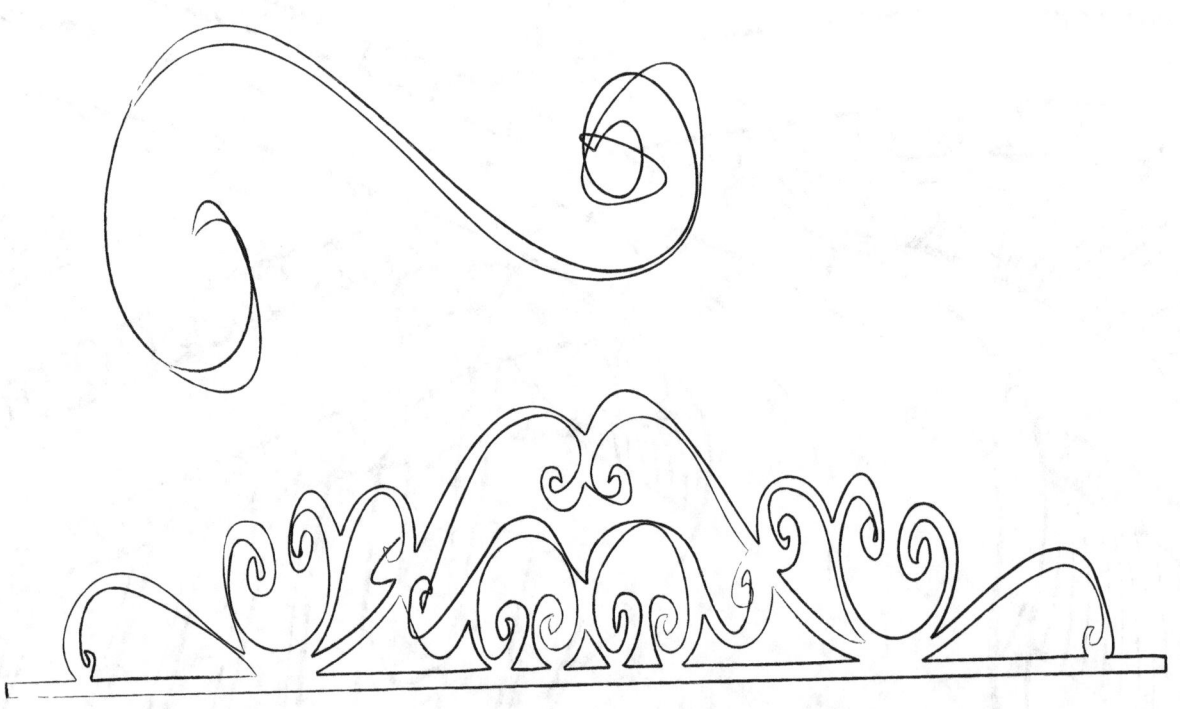

View from the Jackson Street Bridge

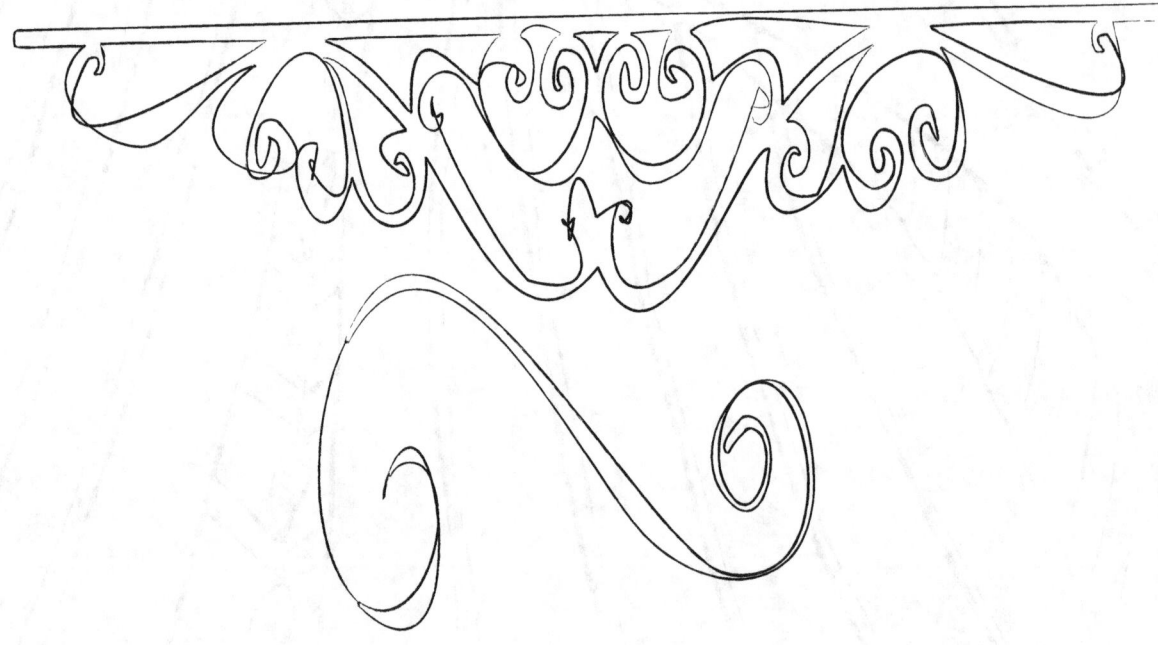

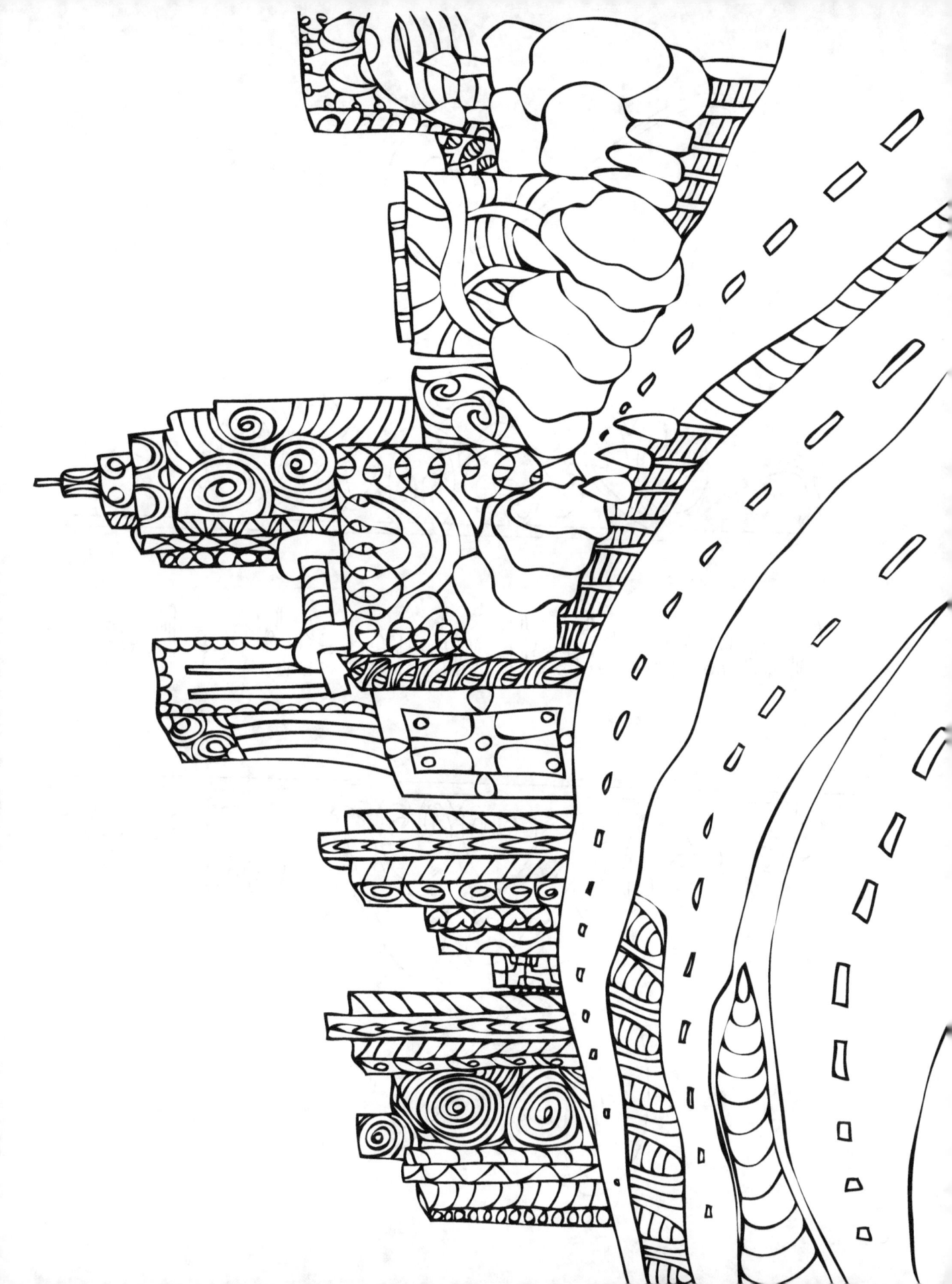

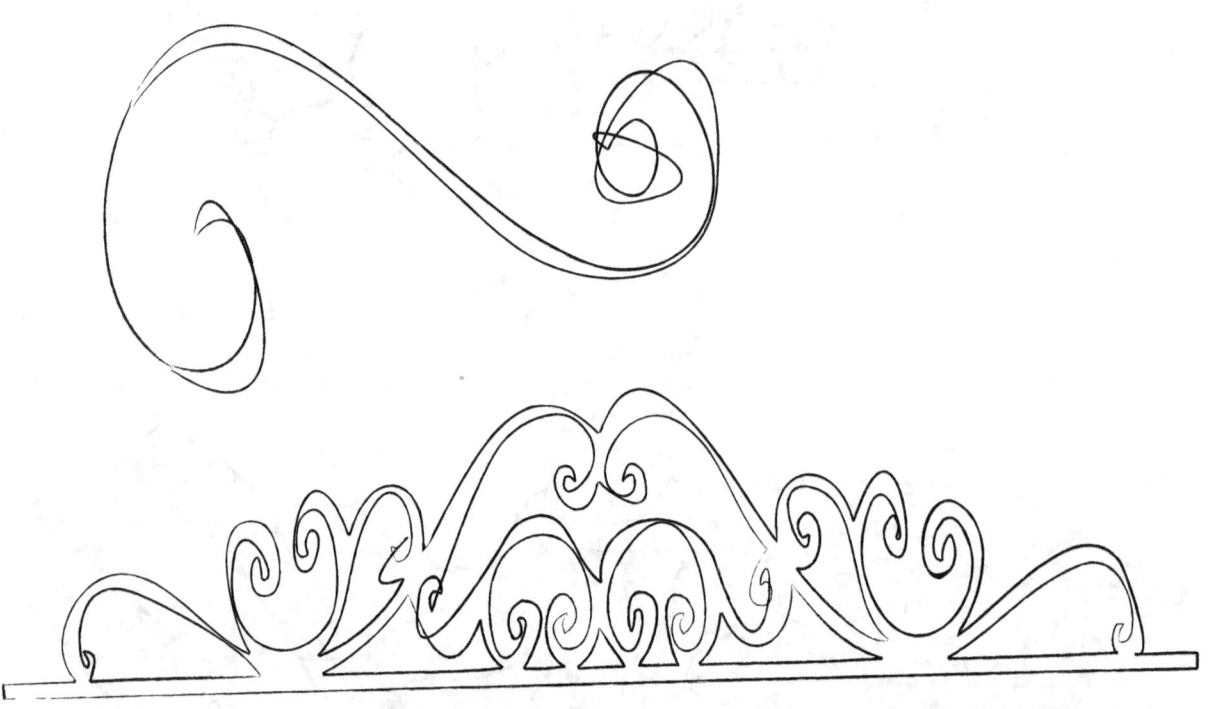

Shows the streets where Peachtree lives

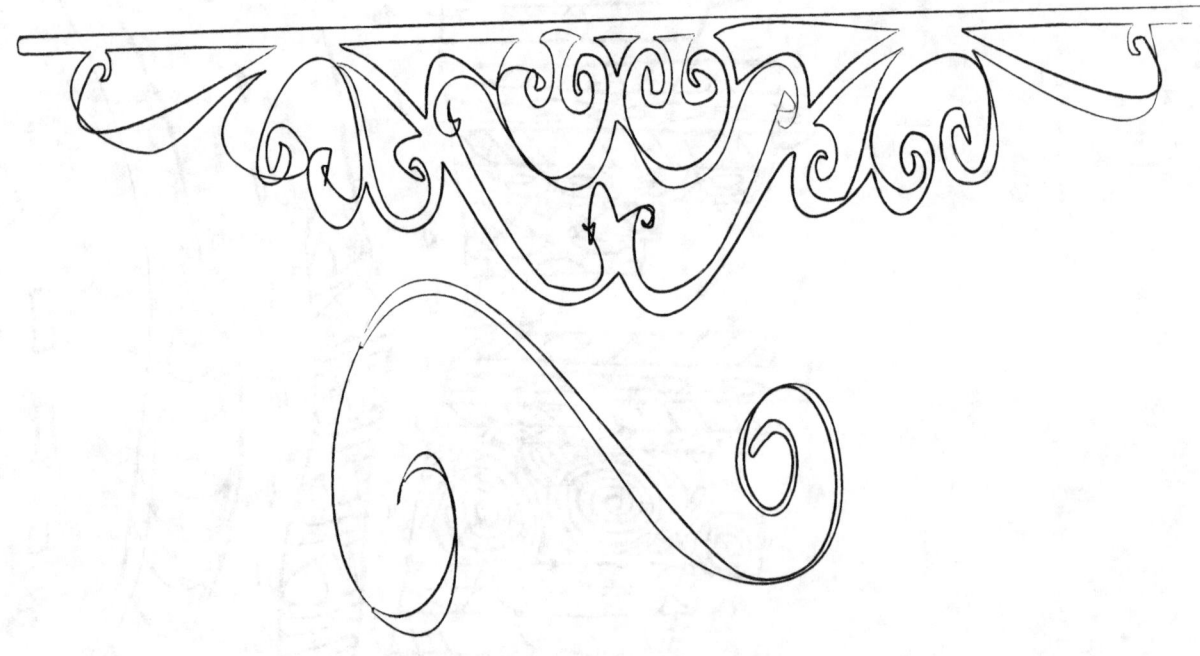

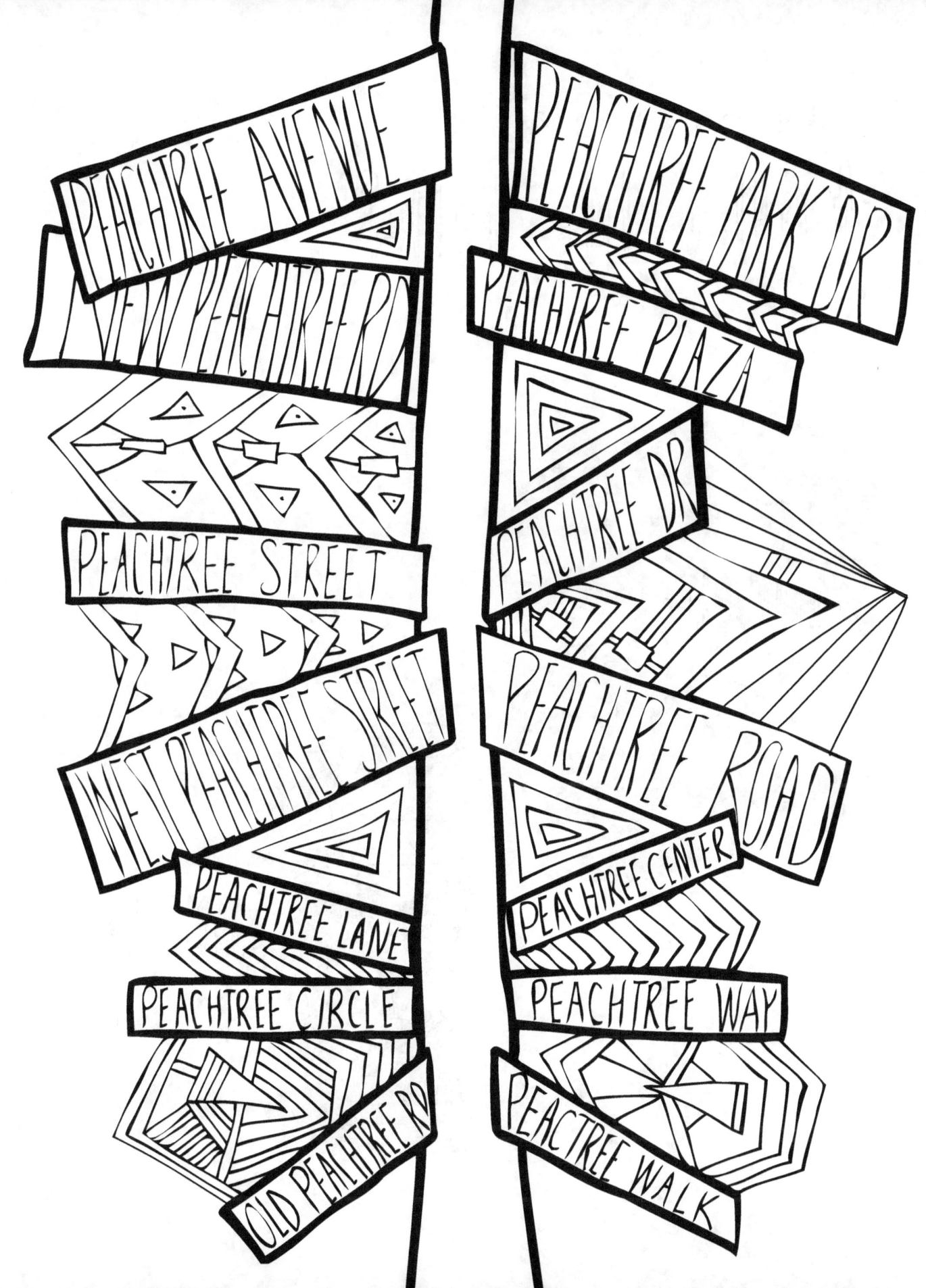

color more from the
doodled life series

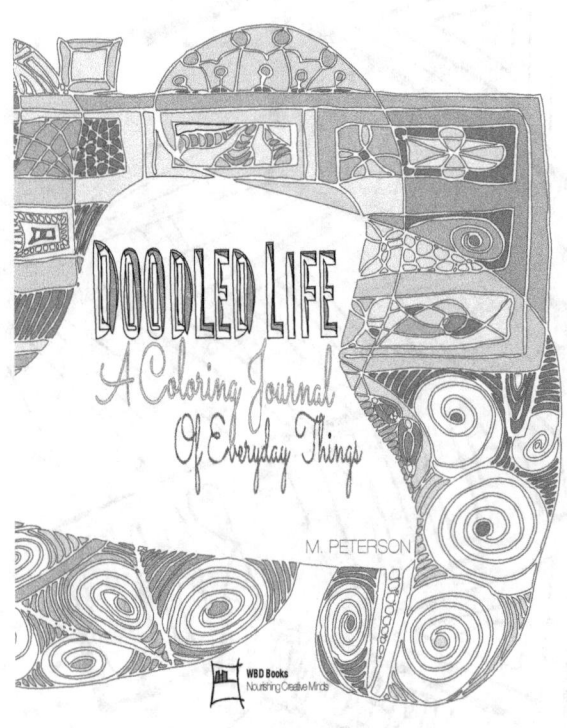

DOODLED LIFE
A Coloring Journal
Of Everyday Things

M. PETERSON

WBD Books
Nourishing Creative Minds

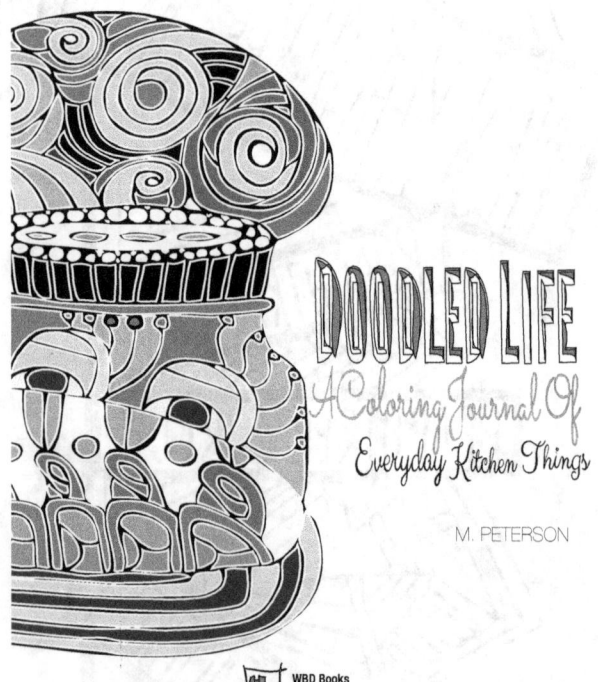

DOODLED LIFE
A Coloring Journal Of
Everyday Kitchen Things

M. PETERSON

WBD Books
Nourishing Creative Minds
WBDBooks.com